Fifty Movies Made

Lessons Learned on a Filmmaker's Journey

∞

By Jared Cohn

DISCLAIMER

This is my memoir, and while everything written here happened as I remember it, the timeline of events is not as linear as it may appear. Life is not linear. Movies and events overlapped. I did my best to arrange my story like a movie schedule—in the most efficient way. Some identifying information has been altered for legal and privacy reasons.

Contents

Foreword

This is an industry with an average lifespan of a gnat. Friends that hit it big struggle after a few years because they are yesterday's headline. A <u>successful</u> career of forty years will yield about fifteen movies—but Jared has been doing this for half as long and made his fiftieth movie before he turned forty.

So, how? How does someone manage to do the impossible? Luckily, you have a master instructor, filmmaker, and entrepreneur in Jared Cohn.

Throughout this book, Jared is going to present some of his more challenging real-world production issues and tell you how he solved the problem. Simple, right? Kinda. Here are two things you need to know:

1. Every show is different. Every problem is different, with one hundred different solutions. The takeaway from this book is that you will encounter problems every minute of the day, and this is one way to deal with them.

2. You're not Jared. Jared is Jared. You will have to figure out the diva moments, the high drama, the accidents, the loss of a location, all on your own. But to understand Jared's methodology, you need to understand Jared.

As a producer, when I see that something is impossible, my go-to director is Jared Cohn. I sent him to Thailand when we had no resources to direct LOCKED UP. I called him up to direct SHARK SEASON, our first show during COVID, to see if it could be done.

I had him direct our first in-house TV series, DISASTER STRIKE FORCE, because the challenge was to do each episode in a few days. When I explain confines to a show (time, location, budget, diva stars)—it's always met with, "When to do we start?" He never complains about anything. He rolls with the drama and finds his own way through.

Add in his personality: Jared is chill. Yeah, yeah…I understand that if someone did fifty films, the assumption is that they are amped, compulsive, perhaps borderline crazy, but Jared…he's chill. Which makes him a threat on the set. You don't see it coming. He is flexible in his method, but incredibly surgical in his execution. He knows what he wants and is unflappable in getting his way.

Sprinkle in the fact that he's smart—chess master smart.

Lastly, he exudes confidence—but in a friendly, non-confrontational way. In short, everyone LIKES him. He's very personable. Very genuine. There is an honesty about him that touches people. He's someone you can approach and collaborate with on a scene. He'll listen to you.

This is Jared's "X" Factor.

And what is your "X" Factor? What is driving you? Every day, you will be tested. You will have self-doubt. You will be challenged. But luckily you have a great teacher who is patient, wise, and funny. Through Jared's mentorship, you will find your "X-Factor" and soon you can approach your next film with, "So…when do we start?"

David Michael Latt
Co-Founder of The Asylum

Preface

This book is for those trying to navigate the bizarre, complex, and competitive film industry where art and profit collide. It's for those seeking wisdom and clarity about what it takes to "make it," those wishing to push forward in their film careers, and those who just want to hear a Hollywood story. These pages contain firsthand knowledge from someone who has spent years in the trenches, trying to figure out this crazy industry.

I am a working movie director, meaning I make movies for a living. I am not an A-list guy. You may not know who I am. But I've directed a lot of movies—fifty and counting—over the past fifteen years. Some of those movies feature stars like Bruce Willis, William Shatner, Mike Tyson, and DMX. Some have even won awards at film festivals, played in theaters across the nation, aired on major networks, and had multimillion-dollar budgets. Other projects had zero funding; it was just me and my camera—no stars.

There have been plenty of ups and downs, and no shortage of crazy shit happened along the way. This book is my story. I hope you enjoy it. And if you learn something, all the better.

Jared Cohn, teenager.

Who I Am

I wasn't the popular kid at Baldwin Public High School. I was kind of an outcast, roaming the prison-styled concrete corridors. Class of 2000, Long Island, New York.

I received mediocre grades, Bs and Cs mostly, because I wasn't interested in anything school had to offer. I did enough to not fail any classes simply because I didn't want to go to summer school or worse, get left behind.

After school, I would rush home, go straight for the TV remote in the kitchen, and watch Kevin Sorbo as Hercules or Lorenzo Lamas in *Renegade*. I'd dream about being them, living their exciting lives. At night, *Star Trek: The Next Generation* was my ultimate jam. I had practically committed every episode to memory. I loved the immersive sci-fi world and wanted nothing more than to fly at warp speed to a galaxy far away and undertake an exciting adventure.

Despite being pretty shy outside of the house, the opposite was true when I was with my family. At home, I made all sorts of weird sounds, did accents, and spun wild stories for my own entertainment. My older brother Jesse and I liked to watch campy karate flicks and mimic the scenes, kicking the shit out of each other. In a way, that was my first "acting" experience.

Both of my parents had creative pursuits of their own when I was growing up. My mother, Karyn Cohn, was a painter and still works as a professional painter to this day. She's a master of her craft, and her work can be seen all over. Growing up, watching her work and seeing her paintings around the house helped me pick up her innate sense of composition. This helped me later understand how to frame a shot and gave me a sense of what is aesthetically pleasing to the eye—a necessary skill for a filmmaker. Every frame is a piece of art or should be.

My father, Steven Cohn, is an amateur photographer who taught me the basics of cameras, lenses, and perspective. I was lucky when DLSRs became video capable because I got to use his extensive sets of Nikon lenses for my projects.

I never thought about what I wanted to do after high school, but my parents wanted me to go to college. Since I had no clue what I wanted to do, I obeyed. My grades weren't great, but they weren't total shit, so I wasn't a total lost cause. After a mass-mailing of applications, I was accepted into Northeastern University's liberal arts program in chilly Boston.

People who don't know what they want to do in life study liberal arts. There's a reason it's called thirteenth grade. There's no specific focus; it's just more high school. You study science, math, English— the same shit as the last four years. And just like I hated high school, I hated liberal arts. I also hadn't considered how damn cold the Boston winter would get. Absolutely miserable weather. I felt awful, like I was wasting my parents' money by not fully applying myself.

During one frigid Boston winter, I was sitting in some sociology lecture when a strange cloud appeared over my head. The professor's voice faded to garbled nonsense, and my heart rate picked up. Reality was smacking me in the face: I was slowly becoming a loser. For the first time in my life, I felt truly hopeless and lost.

Not knowing what you want to do with your life during high school is fine. After high school, not so much. In college, you are literally paying to be there, and paying for something you aren't into is a waste.

I was wasting away with zero purpose in life. By my sophomore year, I moved out of the cramped freshman dorms into a bedroom in an apartment up the street where I met my new roommate, a dark-haired, handsome fellow named DJ Cotrona. I didn't know it at the time, but DJ was different from everyone else at our school. He had bigger ambitions.

DJ was an aspiring actor, and his hobbies were reading movie scripts, studying films, practicing monologues, and communicating with talent agents in Hollywood. It was a fascinating first glimpse into the Hollywood machine, and I wanted to know more. Had I not moved into that apartment and met DJ, I don't think I would be talking about moviemaking at all.

It wasn't long before DJ and I were friends, shooting short comedy skits and watching movies while DJ talked about the actors' performances and other projects. I had never thought of the entertainment industry as an actual industry where people worked. It was all so alien to me, yet DJ had a sound game plan to break into that world. I was impressed—inspired, even.

I would act alongside him in our skits, which was fun for me. But for DJ, it was serious business. Just as my interest in acting was piqued, he told me a talent manager wanted to represent him and that he'd be moving to Los Angeles to pursue acting full time. It was so different from anything I'd seen someone do before and far beyond what I thought I wanted for myself. His move showed me there was more to life than studying something I didn't give a shit about in a place I didn't even like being.

I decided to spend a semester in Los Angeles with DJ, and just as I was preparing to visit, he landed a lead role on a Fox television show, *Skin*. The next thing I knew, I was in LA hanging out with him on a multimillion-dollar set. It was quite the introduction to Los Angeles.

There on the Fox lot in sunny Southern California, surrounded by film equipment, actors, executives, and crew, I fell in love with Hollywood. It was marvelous. I didn't want to leave. I was in love with the business and even more in love with Los Angeles.

Watching DJ perform was all I needed to get bitten by the acting bug for real. I watched the TV production and saw all the elements of escapism laid out in front of me. Fake walls, fake skies, adults playing make-believe. Being on a set made perfect sense to me, and I wanted to be part of it. I wanted to create escapism.

Returning from LA to a freezing geology class taught by a bored professor was all I needed to see my path forward. I needed to get the hell out of Boston and back to Los Angeles. I had never felt motivated to chase a career, but now I was laser focused.

My family thought I was an idiot when I told them I wanted to become an actor, but I wasn't looking for their approval. My older, more financially stable brother, Jesse, suggested I become an FBI agent instead. Agent Cohn sounds pretty rad, and maybe that would've been the more practical decision. But I had come off the Fox lot high, and my friend was a TV star. I knew it was possible— I had seen it firsthand. My family pointed out the high probability of failure, but I held on to my unwavering confidence that things would somehow work out.

I took a page from DJ's playbook and devoured movie scripts. I knew I needed to learn to act properly if I wanted a chance, so I signed up for a class I found in Boston.

Go Write, Go West

L ate one night, I was sitting in my cold studio apartment, with a spliff burning in the ashtray and a cheap glass of whiskey on my desk, when I felt a burst of creative energy. I was midway through reading the script for *Dead Poets Society* on Drew's Script-O-Rama, and something pushed me to open a blank Word document. Right then and there, I started writing my first script.

Story, plot, and characters flowed in from the corners of my mind like a tide. I hadn't studied screenwriting at all, but I'd read enough scripts to think I could do it. Setting and dialogue came pouring out of me, and the more I leaned in, the clearer the story became. This freshman effort would lead to my first complete but still unproduced script, an action screenplay called *Ten Minutes In*. The script is about two friends who try to hit a big score but end up pissing off a drug-dealing gangster and get caught up with crooked cops.

I was already afflicted by the acting bug, but that night, the writing bug came for me. After that, I tuned out of everything else. My classes at Northeastern didn't matter because I was writing a movie script and preparing to tackle Hollywood as an actor. I used the biggest marker I could find to circle the date I planned to leave for the West Coast: August 22, 2002.

I was ready to go west and never look back. Most folks take a week or two to drive across the country, but I got in my Acura Integra and sped from New York to Los Angeles in two days. Outside of getting gas and eating at Waffle House, I didn't stop. I was too excited to start my new life.

At this point, DJ was good friends with movie star Garrett Hedlund and was living at Garrett's place while he filmed *Troy* with Brad Pitt. The plan was that I would join DJ at Garrett's place in Silver Lake, which is quite the Hollywood welcome. During the day, I hung out on the set of a major Fox TV show with Olivia Wilde and DJ, and at night I'd find myself out at Hollywood nightclubs, partying with young celebs like Lindsay Lohan.

But the glitzy welcome to Los Angeles was probably the worst thing that could have happened to me. At the time, I thought it was awesome, but being surrounded by rising stars when you've just landed makes it seem all too easy. I hung out for a better part of a year and started thinking that if I just hung around long enough, I would be successful too. Well, that's not how it works. The glamour fades when everyone around you is talking about working on set and you have nothing to contribute to the conversation other than a "That sounds cool." I didn't want to be a hanger-on any longer — hell, I couldn't afford to be one — so I left. I got my own place and realized if I wanted to work for real, I had to start at the bottom like everyone else.

While taking an acting class might be good training for local theater in Boston, I wanted to be a film and TV actor in LA. I needed to compete with a million other guys just like me, not to mention the ones who were taller or better looking, or who had famous parents.

I needed to enroll in the best acting program I could if I wanted to have any real chance in this town. After some searching, I discovered the two-year Meisner program at the Baron Brown Studio in Santa Monica. This would later help me communicate with actors on set as a director, but at the time, I was certain it was my ticket to stardom.

New Plan

For years, I chased the dream of being an actor. I took every chance, every audition, and although I shot for the stars, I never landed anywhere other than some low-budget sets.

At twenty-three, I was living the actor life in west LA, constantly taking classes and getting new headshots. I had landed the lead in a low-budget horror movie called *Blood Predator* that was filming in Yosemite, California. When I wasn't playing Zak, the stoner who gets killed by aliens, I was studying the camera team, the lighting guys, the art team, and the director. I didn't have any interest in directing yet, but I loved everything about the moviemaking process.

Between shooting scenes and observing the crew, the possibility of getting my action script made toyed with my mind. I tried to chat with the director and producer about it, but they weren't interested. Fortunately, being on location meant late-night hangouts with the cast and crew, and I became friends with the sound guy, a brilliant Russian fellow named Max Nikoff. As fate would have it, Max was also an aspiring director in search of a horror movie to produce and direct.

Max is a genius, and in addition to being an accomplished sound mixer, he is an engineer who served in the Russian army. He captivated me with stories about top-secret missions full of dead bodies and explosions going off around him. We drank Russian vodka and became comrades.

I didn't have a horror script for him, but I told him I could write one. When he asked whether I'd ever written anything, I told him about my action script. He asked to read it so he could get a feel for my writing style and see if we were a good match.

After we wrapped *Blood Predator,* I sent Max the script. To my delight, he complimented my writing style, but that didn't mean he believed I could write a horror script. Eventually, he agreed that if I wrote a good enough script, he would finance and direct it, and I would play one of the main roles. However, if he didn't like the script, nothing would happen. It all sounded good to me, so I took my chances.

Max wanted blood, guts, and boobs—an Uli Lommel–style exploitation movie that could be done on a tight budget. So that's what I wrote.

In my apartment in west LA, I scribbled out *Legend Has It,* a script about a machete-wielding creature who kills a bunch of twenty-somethings. It wasn't my magnum opus, but it was serviceable and could be shot for basically no money. There have definitely been worse sophomore efforts.

Acting as Zak the stoner in Blood Predator.

Legend Has It (2007)

When I first started screenwriting, my process was bizarre and unhealthy. Somehow, I developed this belief that I had to enter some ethereal mindset to be creative. Channeling my inner Hemingway, I would drink and smoke weed to get in the zone.

Without any formal screenwriting lessons to speak of, I read a bunch of finished scripts and how-to books to learn the technique. Looking at a blank screen made my mind grind to a halt, so the alcohol and weed became tools to combat mental resistance. Who was I to write a movie script, especially one that needed to be shot in a single location? I had no experience working with those kinds of limitations. The constant torment and self-doubt drove me to drink more just to write more. I convinced myself I needed this because I didn't think I was a real writer. The worst part is it worked.

All the nonstop writing and drinking meant I was also eating like shit and sleeping even worse. I would plant myself in front of my laptop, drink, smoke weed, eat food from a can, and draft for up to twenty hours at a time. Sometimes I'd go for days on end until a blistering headache took me out. I was so convinced that my writing was shit that I'd delete whole chunks of work to start over. This unhealthy writing process went on until I felt I had a strong enough draft for Max. I was nervous about sharing it because if he didn't like the script, the movie wouldn't be made.

After looking it over for the thousandth time, I sent it off and waited. Every writer knows the gnawing anxiety of waiting for feedback. Imagine working so hard on something, knowing you might just be told, "It's not gonna happen." I've been crushed like that a few times—it doesn't feel great. But this time I was lucky. Max was pretty happy with what I wrote, and *Legend Has It* got the elusive green light.

As soon as we revised and locked in the script, we started talking about locations, casting, props, permits, and everything else it would take to make this movie. It suddenly struck me what an undertaking organizing an entire production would be. It was just the two of us, but we were determined to make the shoot happen no matter what. We traveled across the city, scouting houses to film in, dealing with permit offices and creature designers, purchasing props, and planning the shoot. After a few weeks of prep work, Max offered me a coveted producer credit that I gladly accepted. The title further fueled my passion to make *Legend Has It* the best it could be.

I hadn't set out to become a producer, but if I hadn't put in the effort, the movie wouldn't have come together. So I did whatever I had to do. I didn't really think of it as producing—I was just doing what Max needed to make the movie work.

When it came time for casting, I posted a notice on various websites that I had used as an actor. I booked a theater, went through the headshots, and scheduled audition appointments. Taking on a lot of the leg work was a great learning experience. I knew what it was like as the actor auditioning for the role, but now I was on the other side of the table.

Excited, I told my actor friends that I was making a movie, and they all wanted in. This brought a newfound pressure as I realized casting decisions could affect my relationships with any one of them. So I did what most filmmakers do when they start out: I pushed to cast my friends and girlfriend in the film. In the end, we settled on a combination of my friends and a selection from the auditions.

Neither Max nor I had a clue how to create proper call sheets or schedules, but we cobbled something together in a word-processing program. It detailed which scenes we were going to shoot on what day, where filming would happen, what time we were starting, and when we needed each actor. It was simple, but it got the job done.

Other than securing permits for a few film locations, we did everything else the wrong way. We didn't know any better. This was guerrilla filmmaking. I had been on a lot of sets as an actor, but I didn't know shit about producing. The whole shoot was very DIY, but that was the only kind of production we could afford.

We piled Max's equipment into my car and drove to the 1950s manor we'd booked in Pasadena. After numerous trips where we packed our cars with decorations and props, we went to work decorating the house with cobwebs and moving furniture to make it look as haunted as possible. There was no art department, just Max and me.

The night before filming started, I was nervous as shit. When my alarm went off at five, I had barely slept. Still, I got up and drove to the location house. Despite the bad sleep, I managed to be enthusiastic and energetic, the type of rallying only a young guy can do. When the cast started filing in, Max and I looked at each other and realized we had better get to work.

Max went off to set up the camera and the lights, so I communicated his vision when it came to blocking the first scene. It was never my intent to help direct, but with no other crew on set, I stepped in to assist. Before long, Max and I got into a rhythm where we would talk through the scene, and then he would set up the shot while I worked with the cast. Despite my increased responsibility, I always deferred to Max and made sure he felt respected as the director, because that's what he was.

After trying an emotional, artistic approach with the actors, it was clear that style was not getting us anywhere. Getting into deep discussions of character motivation is too lengthy a conversation when you're already on set. It quickly became clear that it was better to give literal direction. Instead of talking to actors about what they were feeling or thinking, I gave them step-by-step actions to take. As soon as I made this mental shift from emotion to action, I had a revelation about directing. It didn't need to be complex and emotional. It just needed to happen.

If you boil down directing, it's simply guiding the story through the actors. This direct approach worked until it was time to shoot an action scene with a lot of moving pieces. We had Max, myself, four twenty-something actors, and our creature performer dressed in a DIY werewolf suit in an unkempt backyard in Pasadena. The werewolf mask kept falling in front of the actor's eyes, which made it difficult for him to see what he was doing—more than a little concerning, given the real machete he was wielding. On top of that, it was hot as hell, and this poor guy was head to toe in a fur suit, sweating like a pig.

I had zero idea how to put together a scene where a creature jumps out from behind a tree and kills someone before getting chased off. But Max was behind the camera, focused entirely on the shot, so I was left to tell everyone what to do. I didn't yet understand the science of forced perspective, so I took my chances and staged a sequence where the creature performer would swing the machete, and the actor would back up.

When Max called action, the actors entered the scene, and the creature performer jumped out to swing the machete—but the actor didn't back up. Instead, he leaned forward, and the machete sliced the air right in front of his face, nearly taking off his nose. My heart almost fell out of my chest. I wondered what the newspaper would have read if it had gone worse. "Dumbass filmmaker arrested!" I was much more diligent about set safety after that. But that didn't stop us from taking other risks.

While filming, Max and I sometimes needed shots in locations we didn't have permits for. One instance was a short scene at the beginning of the movie where the cast gets into a car before driving to the haunted house together. I suggested we film it near my apartment because there was a relatively quiet alleyway I thought we could use.

A permit would have cost us money we didn't have, so we decided to risk it without one. As the actors and camera gear started piling up outside my building, I began to get anxious that it was obvious we were filming. When a police car whizzed by our side street, I stiffened up, sure they would come out with guns drawn to shut us down. Nothing happened, but I got a rush breaking the rules a bit.

We may have been sloppy, but Max and I powered through and figured it out. We were getting the movie done scene by scene, and the footage was looking pretty cool. Max, being a professional sound technician, got amazing audio, and the camera shots looked great. The movie had the campy, fun feel Max had been looking for.

At the end of the shoot, Max and I celebrated. We had made a movie with no crew and no clue, but somehow, we still got it in the can.

I felt a brief sense of accomplishment after we wrapped, but it became immediately clear that completing the filming was the easy and fun part. Postproduction is an entirely different beast. It would be years before *Legend Has It* was properly edited and finished. It was frustrating, as I had high hopes and wanted it out faster than we could manage.

Years later, Max finished the movie and found a distributor. Although it came out, it certainly didn't make anyone's career. Regardless, it was a great learning experience. If you want to see it, check out *Legend Has It* at https://jaredcohn.com/movies/.

Main cast of Legend Has It, me in the red shirt, playing Ollie.

All In

With the lessons I learned from *Legend Has It*, I felt as though I had enough experience to make my own movie. So I did what every other struggling wannabe director does: I emptied my bank account and borrowed money from my family to make it happen. I was confident I was ready for this next step, just like I was now confident I wanted to be a movie director. I was all in.

Before anything else, I needed a script. I was still under the assumption that working with a super-low budget meant I should do a horror movie. For some reason, I had the idea that if you want to make a feature film cheap and make money, horror was your best bet.

So I opened my laptop in my cluttered, weed-scented apartment in west LA, determined to write the movie that would launch my directorial career. I had been getting some work as an actor, but I was far from thriving. I'd been in LA for five years at that point, and it had been a blur of auditions, classes, headshots, low-budget movies, and phone calls selling people car auction lists. I'd fed my youth to the Hollywood machine. Some of my old high school friends had gone into real careers and were starting to have kids, while I felt like I was stuck in neutral with the e-brake on.

But my next script was going to be my ticket to the next level. I still hadn't proven my parents or brother wrong, and I was sure this would do the trick.

I took my writing process seriously and poured hours into writing and rewriting the script. A script is and always will be the most important part of a movie. That's just a fact. A movie can look beautiful, and the acting can be top-notch, but if the script sucks, the whole movie will suck.

My script was called *And So They Die* and was about a writer hellbent on revenge after his story gets destroyed by a group of drunk jocks. In reality, the story was about me getting bullied and fighting back. I learned early on that incorporating myself and my lived experience into a script can help a story and the characters have more nuance.

I sent the *And So They Die* script to some friends and made adjustments based on their feedback. The script was full of blood, gore, and nudity because I was told that was what sells. By draft ten, when my brain was fried, I was finally satisfied. *And So They Die* was a script worthy of my finances, so I called it complete.

Just like before, I did a breakdown of everything needed to make the movie—a set, a car, props, wardrobe, and so on—and I would handle it all myself. I would have to. I didn't have the budget for a proper crew.

I designed the wardrobe myself and ordered custom Baldwin High School shirts for the jocks to wear when they got killed. After my time getting picked on by jocks at Baldwin High in Long Island, it felt good to get some revenge. As the baseball jocks celebrated a victory in the movie, a killer would take them out one by one. In hindsight, I wrote out a murder fantasy and then filmed it.

Even though I hated doing the paperwork, I still needed insurance and permits. That meant filling out forms, being on hold, leaving messages, and waiting for people to return calls and emails. This preproduction work taught me that although I could do it all myself, it was a hell of a lot of work for one person. Regardless, I was laser focused. I devoted 100 percent of my time to making *And So They Die* happen.

To secure the permit for the house where I'd film, I needed to hand out flyers notifying neighboring houses within a few hundred feet. I followed the rules and stuffed flyers in mailboxes, wedged them in door frames, and even handed them directly to a few folks. Little did I know these people would want to kill me soon after.

At auditions for *And So They Die*, I was determined to cast actors that were right for the role instead of just casting friends. I had no money to pay them, but being in Los Angeles meant there was no shortage of talented actors willing to work for credit and footage. I certainly did a ton of unpaid work as an actor, so I was comfortable with that dynamic.

Despite directing, I still wanted to maintain an acting career, so I cast myself as the killer. However, I made sure to schedule all my scenes for one day so I could focus on directing.

Without much money for equipment, I hired a cinematographer with their own gear. I knew I wanted to shoot on an HVX200 camera because another low-budget horror movie had used one and found good distribution. If it was good enough for that movie, it was good enough for mine.

After some extensive back-and-forth, I worked out a deal with a cinematographer, Scott, who also agreed to provide production and editing services for an additional fee. At the time, I thought I'd lucked out. I had a solid producer and cinematographer and was feeling good about it. I had hired more crew than we had on *Legend*

Has It, including a special effects artist to handle the blood and gore. I wanted this movie to be gory.

The lead-up to the shoot was stressful. I was convinced if I did this movie well, it would give me the career boost and finances I needed to keep going. The stakes were high. Just like my last movie, I slept like crap before day one. When I got to the set in the morning, I was surprised to see producer and cinematographer Scott had shown up with less than half the equipment I had paid for. I asked where the rest of the gear was and he shrugged me off. I couldn't believe it. As mad as I was, there was nothing I could do except continue to make the movie with what we had. It made for a weird morning.

Despite the gear shortage, the beginning of the shoot went well. The cast was excited and easy to direct, and we managed to capture some simple daytime scenes of the kids arriving at the house. Being the actual director this time, I worked with more conviction. I imposed my sense of composition and blocking in the shots. Having a special effects professional on set also made a huge difference when it came time to film some of the kills. Between prosthetics and blood tubing, we got a great shot of a skull being bashed in with sickening accuracy.

Everything was going well. I was having fun, the cast was in good spirits, and the scenes were well blocked. My directing was efficient, and communication was flowing smoothly. I really loved directing. By the end of day one on *And So They Die,* I knew I wanted to direct for the rest of my life.

The script called for a lot of kills at night, so that meant there would be a lot of screaming when the sun went down. This might not have been a problem elsewhere, but we were shooting in a residential corner of Eagle Rock, California. I told the homeowner it was a horror movie when we booked the property, but I hadn't warned him about the late-night murder scenes. For some reason, I didn't realize it might be a problem.

The house was tucked away with a fairly big backyard, but there were still neighbors within earshot. So when they heard screaming late at night, they did the logical thing: they called the cops. It ended up being the first of many encounters I would have with law enforcement as a filmmaker. Angry, pajama-clad neighbors marched onto the property, screaming about having work in the morning or that their kids couldn't sleep. I felt bad for them, I did, but all my money was tied up in the movie. I had to keep going.

It turned into a mess with the cops asking questions and the neighbors cursing at me. Thankfully, I had the permit on our side, including the notices we'd handed out. Not one of the neighbors had said a thing when they saw the notices beforehand, but now they were complaining we hadn't warned them about the screams. Apparently, I'd left that part out.

The homeowner was freaking out but, to his credit, allowed us to continue filming. He didn't even stop us when his neighbors kept screaming, "Shut the fuck up!" throughout the night. I do hope they eventually forgave him.

After the main cast finished shooting on the final day, we shot my scenes. The pressure was on. In my mind, I had to give my best performance to sell the movie. I went so far as to destroy my old laptop to up the production value for a scene. After my scenes, we wrapped on *And So They Die.*

I was feeling pretty good as I was cleaning up the location, but then came Scott to tell me that most of his equipment had been stolen. I was in disbelief. How could all of this gear just disappear—and on the last day of the shoot? He insisted I file an insurance claim for the stolen gear, but I didn't want to. I thought Scott was trying to pull a fast one on me to make some extra money. He'd shown up on day one with less than half the equipment we agreed on, so I already knew he was not a great guy.

When you're a greenhorn filmmaker, you want to find someone with more experience to help you put everything together. However, if you aren't careful, you are exposing yourself to the many unsavory characters who prey on young filmmakers the second you post that you're looking for crew.

Because our deal included editing services, I eventually went to see his progress after a few weeks. One scene was edited, and very poorly at that. I wanted to take the hard drives back and find a new editor; I also wanted the money that I paid for his editing back. Scott refused to renegotiate and when I got upset, he threatened to delete the footage.

My heart sank. He really had me over a barrel. Either I file an insurance claim for his "stolen" gear and let him keep the editing fee, or he would delete my movie. This was my first movie on my own, and I was being forced to choose between committing insurance fraud or not completing the film at all.

The whole experience left a bad taste in my mouth. It's even worse because Scott was taking advantage of the vulnerability of someone just trying to be creative. Hollywood is notorious for grifters, and there I was, the victim of one on my first movie.

Morality and criminality aside, the reality was I needed the movie done. I had taken money from my family, so failing to make my directorial debut wasn't an option. There was no choice but to move forward, even if that meant defrauding the insurance company.

I filed the claim, which took forever to process through the appropriate channels. In the meantime, I was receiving aggressive texts from this maniac grifter demanding his money and continually threatening to delete footage. After a month of mental torture, I finally got the money from the insurance company, and we arranged a meetup. I gave Scott the check, and he gave me the hard drives. At last, the nightmare was over. Years later, I found out he not only has a criminal record but has pulled the same grift on other filmmakers and now appears to be a squatter. I wasn't surprised to see it.

With my footage back, it was time to edit, and I was determined to do better due diligence when hiring. I found an editor, Ryan, with some solid, verifiable IMDb credits and reached out to a former client for a reference. Eventually, we made a deal.

However, when Ryan and I met, and he finally plugged in the drives, not all of the footage was there. I was so upset. Even the shot of my laptop getting destroyed was missing. How could I have let this happen? Missing shots I knew we had gotten. I was stressed and felt duped by Scott yet again.

Despite not having all the footage, Ryan and I worked on the movie at his house for months. Some scenes came out great, others not as great, but it was a solid movie overall. But when we had to patch up scenes because we were missing footage, my excitement took a turn. Without all the intended shots, it didn't look as good as I wanted it to. I kept ping-ponging between thinking it was a solid movie and a total piece of shit.

The stress of having my movie held hostage and mutilated kept me from focusing on my acting career. This lack of confidence meant I was also struggling to perform at the phone sales job I used to pay the bills, sending me toward poverty and deep into depression.

I looked in the mirror. I was twenty-six, broke, and beaten up by Los Angeles. It seemed like just yesterday I was nineteen, fresh faced, and ready to tackle Hollywood. I had been overconfident, thinking it would be easy. Although I still thought I had a chance at success, my life was passing me by, and all my accomplishments seemed inadequate. I questioned what the hell I was still doing in Hollywood.

Fueled by spliffs and pizza, Ryan and I got through the tedious editing process and managed to put together a pretty cool flick. I hired a composer to score some original music for it, and suddenly I had a completed movie with a snazzy trailer to show for it.

My bank account was withering by the day, and I was eating like shit, drinking too much, and feeling like garbage. I was in a bad way and running out of money to stick around, and the depression that had crawled into my foggy skull was too much for me to handle. I needed to get out of town. I had experienced bouts of depression while trying to make it as an actor, but this was way darker than before. During the day, I was in agony. At night, I couldn't stop ruminating. I couldn't work, I couldn't sleep, and when I realized *And So They Die* wasn't going to launch my career, I was damn near suicidal. I called my family to tell them I was coming back to

New York. After six years of grinding, trying to win in Hollywood, I couldn't take it anymore.

When my mother pulled us into the driveway of my childhood home, I wept like a little kid. I had tried and failed. I was just a statistic.

Schooled

I tried to get into the acting scene in New York shortly after getting home, but I struggled to make connections. Just like in LA, all of my successful auditions led to more low-budget stuff. At one point, I was cast to play the lead in a horror movie, *Feed the Devil,* but it got pushed indefinitely right before filming started. Everything seemed to be falling apart, and I desperately needed work.

After moping around and being a server at a terrible seafood restaurant in Long Island, I was seriously contemplating my future. Should I keep trying to find work in the entertainment industry or just throw in the towel and become a cop?

Since my parents were bummed I ditched college for Hollywood, I decided to go back to school for a degree. I despised the film industry because I didn't understand it, but I still couldn't shake my dream of working in the movies. I remembered how creative and freeing it was to work on set, and I wanted that.

There is no clear road map to success in Hollywood. You could grind for ten lifetimes and still not make a dent, but I couldn't let it go. I loved making movies; I loved the whole process. The times I was filmmaking were the most creative experiences I ever had, so I had to figure out a way to not only stay in the game but win it. I had to succeed. It was that or die.

My parents just wanted me to get a degree. They didn't care too much about what it was in, so when I proposed film school, their response was, "As long as you graduate." That sounded like a yes to me, so film school it was. After transferring some credits from my college in Boston, I enrolled at the New York Institute of Technology, a prestigious four-year institution with campuses in Long Island and Manhattan.

People talk a lot of shit about going to film school. They say Quentin Tarantino and so-and-so didn't go there. I'll admit it, you don't need to go to school to succeed in the industry. I'm not going to say whether or not someone should go to film school. For starters, it's expensive. Besides, you can always start out as a production assistant and move up the ladder that way, but I was lost at the time. I needed structure, and film school sounded interesting. Being a successful working actor would've been nice, but the universe was not bending to my wishes — and I sure as shit wasn't bending the universe to my will.

Positive relationships with good professors make or break the college experience, and I was fortunate to have some great mentors like Professor Sherwin, Professor Fauvell, and Professor Fizzinoglia. These guys have been teaching young filmmakers for years. They spent time in the industry, worked, and now share their knowledge with the next generation.

As I was learning to edit, light, and use a camera, a revelation hit me: if I could learn all of the components of making a movie, I would never get ripped off by people like Scott again.

I decided to commit myself to the technical aspects of filmmaking right then and there, and my new thirst for knowledge propelled me. I was the best film student ever. Not only did I get straight As, but I also did extra work. I rented out the school's equipment every weekend, linked up with music artists, and offered to shoot and edit a music video for free. There were a lot of free music videos back then.

I spent every waking hour in class, watching tutorials online, or practicing my newfound video skills. I subscribed to all the magazines, joined forums online, and did twenty-four-hour film contests. I became a machine.

In addition to my studies, I worked crew with Greg Filipkowski, an amazing filmmaker who was and is the king of commercials on Long Island. I learned a lot from Greg; he would take his time with every frame and wouldn't roll until the picture looked exactly the way he wanted it. He would make the tiniest adjustments to the frame or lighting and practice the camera movements, and his meticulousness showed in his work. Greg used to say, "Do it nice or do it twice." Then he started saying, "Do it nice or don't do it at all." We worked together quite a bit; I assisted with camera and lighting and even starred in a few of the commercials. He helped me learn to take my time with framing, because once you press that red button, there's no going back.

My video skills sharpened over time. I knew the rundown on all the latest hardware and software and kept up with *Videomaker* and *American Cinematographer* to stay informed.

Eventually I stopped making free videos and started a business, Traplight Media. Between school and filming, I went to business networking events at hotels and restaurants to sell people on why they needed a video. By the time film school was wrapping up, I was getting steady work as a one-man video maker in the Long Island suburbs—quite the turn after leaving LA with my tail between my legs.

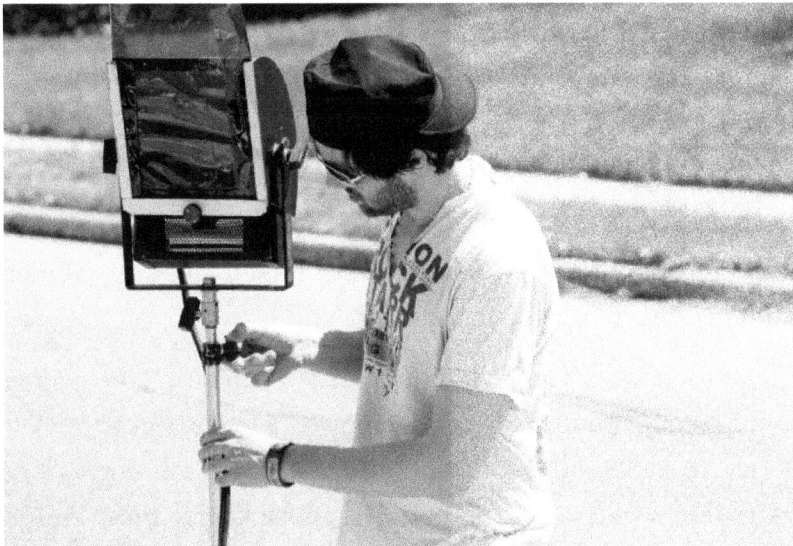

Me as a film student, setting a light for a school project.

Hulk Blood Tapes (2009)

Before graduating from film school, I had to complete my final thesis film for Professor Robert Sherwin's class. Instead of shooting a short film like everyone else, I decided to do a feature-length, found-footage movie. I wanted to push myself.

I came up with an idea for a script about a group of friends, who crash their car on their way to a concert and get stuck in the woods with no phone service, no food, and no supplies. Some real *Deliverance*-type shit.

The characters are en route to a concert by Hulk Blood, a rock band from Long Island. The cast consisted of myself and a few students from film class: Ben, Nikki, and Matt.

Because there wasn't enough time to write a full script, the dialogue was going to be improvised as we followed a beat sheet to track the plot points. In the plot, someone dies after the crash, the cast gets lost in the woods, another person gets sick and dies, and the remaining two are found at the last minute by a person riding by on a horse.

The shoot was set to take place at my dad's house in upstate New York to take advantage of the nearby wooded areas. I rented a camera, mic, and some lights from school, and off we went. We took advantage of the drive from suburban Long Island to rural upstate New York and filmed scenes leading up to the crash. The camera was passed around from person to person as we improvised dialogue until we wound up with more than enough footage for a well-developed setup. The acting was so natural because we were just playing ourselves, teasing each other, and laughing. We stopped for gas and lunch and smoked some weed, capturing it all on camera. When the time finally came, we approached a cliff and prepared for the crash shot.

The interior crash shots were captured by shaking and throwing the camera as we flung ourselves around the moving vehicle. With all our frenetic energy, we sold crash well. We watched the playback of the shot, and it really did look like the car could be falling down a cliff. We tossed stuff around and screamed loud enough to create the illusion.

The next thing we needed was a shot of the car after the crash. Thankfully, we'd secured a junker for the occasion. I remember it being towed in by my dad's buddy while we stood at the top of a steep cliff, anxious and excited at the thought that we were going to watch the car tumble. This felt like big-budget moviemaking stuff even though we were just film students.

The only game plan we had to get the car to the bottom of the cliff was to shove it. It was the easiest way. We lined the nose up so it pointed right down the cliff, and I waited for someone, anyone, to jump out and stop us because we didn't have a permit. But we were in upstate New York. Nobody was around, and we were free to do whatever we wanted.

Nervously, the cast placed their hands on the trunk of the car next to mine. I was determined to send it straight to the bottom. I needed it to because I had a movie to shoot, and we were losing daylight. With everyone poised, I counted down from three and pushed.

The car rolled right off the edge and down the rocky hill. I watched as it suddenly picked up speed, went over a boulder, and veered off course, smashing into a tree halfway down the cliff. I was devastated. This wasn't going as planned. The car had to land at the bottom of the cliff for the story to work how I had envisioned it, but instead it was wrapped around a tree. The worst part was the sun was going down fast. I bit back the failure that welled in my stomach and gritted my teeth. Failure wasn't an option here.

There had to be a way to remedy the issue. I insisted there was a way to free the smashed car and get it down the cliff. But the cast was unconvinced. People were telling me it was impossible and that I could hurt myself. But I didn't want to hear any of that. If no one else would, I was going to make it down the cliff to the car.

With all eyes on me, I made the trek down to the car and pushed with all my might. It didn't budge, not an inch. Everything was riding on this, so I gave the car one more push and ended up falling instead. I tripped on a log and busted my ass before tumbling down to the bottom of the cliff.

People called out, asking if I was okay. The question alone implied I wasn't, but I kept a brave face as I wiped blood off my hand and assured them I was fine. The worst part wasn't the physical pain—it was the thought of losing the shot. For days I had pictured the smashed car at the bottom of the cliff. It needed to be there! I refused to give up, so I trekked back up the cliff, grabbing onto trees on the way.

At the top, I looked for a chain, thinking we could attach it to the car and pull it up with another vehicle and drop it again.

We had a pickup truck, so I thought it wouldn't be a problem, and for once I was right. We were able to free the junk car from the tree, cut the chain, and watch it roll down and land with a boom exactly where I wanted. I was so relieved. It was an ambitious idea, maybe not as well thought out as it could've been, but we made it work. I was on cloud nine. The pain and bruises from falling down hurt less once I knew we could continue shooting as planned.

After the crash, the cast trekked into the woods, away from the crash site, just as the sun was going down. It was cold, and my costar and film school classmate, Matt Neglia, was filming us complaining in character. We were genuinely cold and uncomfortable, so the complaining came naturally.

We set up camp and lit a fire in the midst of some trees. It didn't take long for the camera to become an observer as we immersed ourselves in telling jokes and stories. It was funny and felt real. Some of the things we said were way wittier than anything I could've written. With *Hulk Blood Tapes*, I caught a glimpse at how awesome improv could be.

Our characters journeyed through the woods and survived wild animals, illness, and a lack of water. By the end, I had plenty of found footage to work with, and I knew how to edit by myself. I would not hand a red cent over to anyone to complete this movie. I was going to do it all—editing, sound, music, and titles. I was proud I had the technical proficiency to do it and didn't need to depend on grifting fraudsters.

Editing was still new and exciting, so I worked nonstop and finished a one-hundred-minute cut in just a few weeks. The class liked my movie, and I walked away with an A+.

Go see it for yourself at https://jaredcohn.com/movies/. It's not bad for a guy in film school.

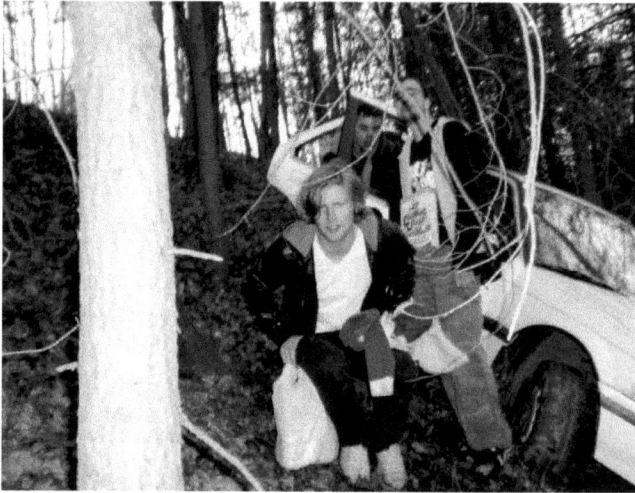

On set of Hulk Blood Tapes.

Film school graduation with Professor Jim Fauvell, New York Institute of Technology, Class of 2010.

Underground Lizard People (2010)

In 2010 my father's friend Ron wanted to make a low-budget movie, and my dad was kind enough to point him in my direction. Luckily, Ron was for real and had a few bucks to spend on production. *Hulk Blood Tapes* had just wrapped, and I was still finishing school, but I couldn't turn down an opportunity to make a movie I didn't have to pay for. In fact, I would actually earn some money this time.

My excitement helped me recruit the cast and crew from film school along with a camera operator I met working on local commercials. The movie was about underground lizard people, a subject Ron was highly passionate about for some reason. Who was I to argue? I didn't know anything about lizard people, but I was about to learn because I was tasked with penning the screenplay. I negotiated a deal with Ron, and off I went to research whatever I could.

Educating myself on lizard people became crucial during early development conversations. Ron would talk about things I had no context for, so I would go online and dive into all things humanoid reptile. I read theories from offbeat writers about murders with witnesses who claimed the killers were lizard-like. Some obscure websites included maps and weird videos about underground cities hidden next to actual abandoned railways. There was no shortage of theories about lizard people living on earth. Some even suggested prominent leaders were among them. Other theories detailed a subculture of people who drank blood and killed babies. The internet took me down a rabbit hole with all kinds of tunnels, so I had a lot of options to work with.

Needing to narrow my scope, I asked Ron which story elements were important to him. I needed to do my best to understand his motivation for making this movie if I wanted my script to satisfy. Since the crux of the story would be where the lizard people lived, I showed him one of the rail maps I'd found online, and he agreed that these lizard people likely resided in the railway system. At least I had that part nailed down.

As we fleshed out the plot, we landed on a rather simple storyline. A group of researchers stumbles upon a nest of lizard people, and the lizard people kill them. Truth is, I didn't know what else lizard people would do if they were discovered, so killing the scientists made the most sense. After Ron agreed, we dove into what the lizard people would look like and how they would kill their victims. It turns out lizard people sightings have been going on for hundreds of years, and what people say they look like is anything from a normal human to a giant lizard to a person with scales. Since this would be a horror movie, I suggested that the lizard people look as scary as possible on a low budget.

Once we were finally on the same page regarding the kind of movie he wanted to make and what we could actually afford, I began the screenwriting process. The outline was printed out and taped to my wall while I had my computer open to a blank document. After defeating my urge to procrastinate by suddenly cleaning my room, I hunkered down and wrote, eyes focused, fingertips dancing on the keyboard.

Anyone who has written a lengthy document knows the feeling of staring at a screen until your eyes glaze over, your fingertips hurt, and your brain aches. There is zero glamour in writing. You're hunched over a screen pressing buttons, just as I am doing right now. It's taxing on your brain and body. Days and weeks can pass in a blur, and the only thing that changes is how many words are written. Thankfully, I was past the phase of thinking I had to be drunk or stoned to be creative, so I powered through by sheer will.

After Ron read the first draft, we met at a coffee shop on Long Island, and I took down as many notes as I could. After some back-and-forth, I was able to nail down his biggest concern. He wanted to make sure the main location, the habitat, would look good since the majority of the movie would take place there. He also asked if it would be possible to find an abandoned railway to shoot at, which he, of course, would have to approve of.

Not knowing any better, I assured him it wouldn't be a problem. The next few weeks consisted of a thousand unanswered phone calls and emails. Finding an abandoned railway in New York that would allow us to film was going to be a much bigger challenge than I had anticipated, and since the majority of the movie took place there, it needed to be cinematic. We called every railway we could, but none of them would allow us to shoot there—or they would, but it would have cost too much on our low budget.

After exhausting almost every company I could think of, one kind government rail worker showed interest in what we were up to. This kind fellow referred me to a freight company that owned a section of railroad reserved for loading cargo. I called the company, and thankfully the boss was a film lover. We spoke about movies, and he was very accommodating and interested in our production. The owner gave Ron and me a grand tour of his rail section, half of it above ground and the other half underground. It was perfect! And thankfully, Ron agreed to the location.

I am still shocked we found a railroad location, let alone a section with an active Brooklyn railroad tunnel. The owner told us that when trains came through, they would be slow, so even if a train was coming at us, we would have plenty of time to get out of the way. The notion of us filming and a train blazing through the set definitely put a little fear into me, but this was our only option, so I signed the location deal.

The trains did come, and we had to move our gear around to accommodate them, but they stayed on schedule, and thankfully nobody got hurt.

I still hadn't gotten rid of the actor bug, so I cast myself in this movie as well. This time it was a mistake. My part was not written to be filmed on a day when it would be easy to work around my other responsibilities. It was a big supporting role, so I had to direct one moment and then jump into wardrobe and makeup the next. I was directing scenes in costume as a half-human, half-lizard hybrid, but when my focus shifted to acting, people grew frustrated with the lack of direction. It's hard to get into character, perform well, and still direct and produce.

At one point we were trying to shoot a scene where a researcher wanders off and then gets himself killed. A location had been selected during preproduction, and when it came time to light the scene, the crew wanted me to verify certain details before setting up the lights. But I was nowhere to be found. Instead of being available, I was sitting in my car across the set, practicing my upcoming lines.

I had assumed everyone knew the location, but wanting to confirm with the director before hauling equipment is normal. By the time someone found me, we had lost a lot of time, and people were getting frustrated.

Another scene required extensive makeup on my face, as my character was being revealed as a lizard person. Actors arrived to block the scene, and afterward I went back to makeup. But the actors had more questions. It's impossible to answer blocking questions when you are sitting in the makeup chair. As I looked at myself in the lit mirror, I realized I was not being a good director.

The worst part was that when I got to set, some of the actors and crew had decided to change the blocking in a way that didn't fit the film, leaving me with the terrible task of having to undo their changes. It was a disaster, and being dressed up as a lizard person certainly didn't help me assert my vision.

A director is supposed to be the captain of the ship, the person people look to for answers. If the director is absent, unfocused, or doesn't know what they are doing, chaos breaks out. It's like a class without a teacher. Questions go unanswered, nobody is responsible, and nothing gets done.

There's a learning curve to becoming a movie director. At first you suck because you've never done it before. And even though I had directing credits, I sucked on that shoot. I had let the movie get away from me. I wasn't engaging as the director. I wasn't taking initiative. I was busy acting.

When that revelation dawned on me, I took control. We rewrote the script on the fly, cutting my scenes so I could focus on directing. I felt stupid for even casting a part for myself. A real director would have never done such a thing, I was sure.

We got through the shoot and loaded our equipment up on the dark train tracks for the last time. At home in my bedroom, I edited half of the movie before the cinematographer cut the rest. It turned out pretty cool. But cutting my scenes came with its own repercussions. The final cut was only seventy-five minutes of a movie, and that wasn't good. To get distribution as a feature-length film, you need eighty-five to ninety minutes at minimum. There is no hard rule, but I wouldn't feel right calling a seventy-five-minute movie a feature.

I wrote new pages and found a location for free to shoot fifteen minutes of new run time.

Adding pages to a short movie is hard because the scenes are essentially just fluff. You can try and make them work to flesh out characters or create a subplot, but it's hard to make them not feel tacked on. After *Underground Lizard People*, I always made sure I had enough run time to keep the movie from coming in short. That said, it happens. Reshoots happen; pickup days are sometimes necessary. Will a producer ever be happy to spend more money to finish a movie? No. But will they blame the director? Always.

Underground Lizard People finished as a fun, campy project. We got it done on schedule and on budget. The original cut is available at https://jaredcohn.com/.

Around the same time we finished *Underground Lizard People*, I graduated film school. It felt good. Now I had a fancy piece of paper to show people if they asked. But nobody did, not even once. Still, I felt accomplished and even graduated cum laude. At the very least, my parents were proud.

After that, I busied myself shooting videos or working crew. If I wasn't doing that, I was screenwriting. I was reinvigorated. Now that I didn't have to go to class, I could hunker down to write script after script after script.

Directing while acting in Underground Lizard People.

Born Bad (2011)

By 2011, my writing process sped up so that what once would've taken me several months, I could now do in three weeks, if I focused. So I focused. I hunkered down, and I wrote. Armed with my scripts, I started pitching, hoping I could get one made into a movie.

The Asylum is a prolific production company that I encountered during my time as an actor. They're the geniuses responsible for *Sharknado*, and if you haven't heard of that movie, you must live under a rock.

I had previously been cast in four Asylum movies, so I thought I might have a shot at getting the partners to read one of my scripts. The one I was most proud of was a horror movie called *Steady Denny*, which I had completed during an alcohol-, weed-, and caffeine-fueled writing blitz. As I had in other scripts, I wrote the title role, Denny, for myself. The characters I wrote for myself were always the most fleshed out and interesting, probably because I knew myself better than anyone else. Writing the role for myself also allowed me to dig deeper and ask myself questions about motivation and character action. I would later use this trick much more frequently, often putting myself into several roles in the same script to develop better characters.

I sent *Steady Denny* to David Rimawi, a partner at The Asylum. Rimawi is a very busy man, making over twenty movies a year, so getting him to read a spec script wasn't going to happen overnight.

And it didn't. It wasn't until months later when I was having dinner with my dad that I got a call from LA.

I was ecstatic to hear that David read the script and liked it.

"Can you come to the office Thursday to discuss?" he asked.

It was Tuesday, and I was still in New York, but I told him I'd be there and set a time. I did not tell him I was across the country. I didn't want to give him a reason to postpone the meeting.

Getting an actual meeting is a big deal. Single meetings have changed countless lives in the industry. An elusive "real" meeting is far different from the usual "we should meet up sometime" or "let's link up to discuss." If you think you have a meeting, but there's no set time, date, or location, guess what? They probably don't like your project and just don't want to tell you to your face. Any answer other than a yes is a no.

On Thursday, I sat across from Rimawi in his executive office, in Burbank, California, where most of the major studios are. Movie posters from Asylum classics like *King of the Ants* and *Intermedio* lined the walls, while directors and actors buzzed around the place. The Asylum was in business, and I was glad to be there, excited about life again. Even better, David Rimawi said *Steady Denny* could be right for a Lifetime thriller. He wanted to change the name to *Born Bad*, and the violence would have to be toned down, but a proper made-for-TV movie was a big step up from the tiny budget stuff I was doing back in New York. I was excited to be leveling up.

At the same time, David also explained that if I wanted to play the lead, the budget would be set much lower since I had zero star power. However, if I wanted to direct, they would cast star names.

I had not directed a movie with an actual star actor yet, but choosing between directing star names and starring in a low-budget movie was still pretty tough at the time. Part of me still wanted to be an actor, and I thought if I performed well enough in *Born Bad*, it could launch my acting career. There were periods when I made some decent money as an actor in LA, but reality reared its head to remind me that I was no star. It was a jagged pill to swallow, but I had no other choice.

The chance to direct stars with a real budget was too good to pass up. I told him I was happy to stay in the director's chair for this one.

I was all smiles until Rimawi asked me if I had ever directed anything before. Thank God I had taken out all my money to make *And So They Die* because I could at least show him that. But what if he didn't like it? Would he retract the offer and crush my dreams on the spot?

I popped the DVD for *And So They Die* into his computer and showed him the most exciting scenes and gory kills. To my relief, he smiled. He liked what he saw and wouldn't be snatching away the director's role. Without *And So They Die*, there's a good chance I would not have been offered the directing position. He easily could have bought the script and hired another director.

Everything was moving along nicely until Lifetime was sent the script. Notes came in. A lot of notes. Suddenly, what I thought was a sure thing was up in the air.

The original script I wrote for *Born Bad*, the script formerly known as *Steady Denny*, capitalized on violence. In it, Denny murders a series of people in ways that were too violent for a made-for-TV movie. It wasn't written to be a TV movie after all; it was written as a horror movie. However, this project had to be a thriller, and that meant some violence was fine—but the draft was too much.

I froze looking over all the notes. I couldn't process the amount of work ahead of me. I wanted to cry. There was no way I would be able to incorporate all of the feedback into my story. These were not simple, easy-to-do changes. They were expecting major character revisions that would affect the entire script. I was overwhelmed and didn't know where to start drafting. For the next few days, I stared at my screen, read the notes, looked back at the script, and wondered how I could make a bad character more likable or the father character more proactive. Some of the notes were written so vaguely I felt like I was solving a riddle.

One note simply read, "We need to care more about the girl before she gets killed." That could be accomplished a million ways, but only a few would be the "right way." The only good thing about obsessing over a script is ideas will come to you when you least expect them. I could be in bed, just about to fall asleep, when another idea would spring me out of bed. Back to my computer to dive right in.

Another note was to delay the bad guy's reveal, but I thought one of the murders was necessary to establish the antagonist. Every other note was understandable, but I felt strongly enough about this one to fight. I had been working nonstop on the other notes, so I thought I had a chance at standing my ground. I put together a long email, taking painstaking measures to make my case, only to get a quick response insisting I comply. Although I felt defeated, the fact I was making a real movie helped me shut up and listen to the note.

If someone is willing to invest real money into turning your words into a movie, you work for them, and you should be grateful for the chance. Make the notes work. If you try to game them by only doing a few, it will come back to bite you. People who read scripts for a living are smarter than that.

Micho Rutare is one of those smart script readers and was the head of development at The Asylum during preproduction for *Born Bad*. Micho helped me interpret the notes and find creative ways to incorporate them into the script.

The moment the script was finally approved was such a relief. The start date was set, and I was anxious but ready.

The Asylum put together a star cast of Michael Welch (*Twilight*), David Chokachi (*Baywatch*), Meredith Monroe (*Dawson's Creek*), and Bonnie Dennison (*Third Watch*). When I heard those were the names I would be directing, my entire career felt validated. The thought of it was unreal. I almost felt like asking if they were sure about the decision. It was humbling. I knew who these actors were—I had watched them on TV! I was excited but also nervous. I didn't want to fuck it up.

I remember feeling a little jealous of Michael Welch because I had written the lead role for myself, but he played Denny better than I would've, and he brought star power. I made peace with the world never seeing my rendition of Denny because it meant I was a real movie director now, not an actor who hadn't quite made it.

Since we were working with stars, *Born Bad* was associated with the Screen Actors Guild (SAG). Making a SAG movie is a big deal for a new director because SAG productions are much more regulated. There are rules to protect the actors and make sure they are fed and paid on time, as well as other requirements you wouldn't find on a non-SAG set.

Born Bad being SAG associated meant it was more of a "real" movie, and that added to both my nervousness and excitement.

Guerrilla filmmaking was all I knew until that point. I could shoot, edit, and deliver a video, and thanks to film school, I knew the technical ins and outs. But I had never worked with a real schedule or production team, and no film school can teach you how to direct stars with a full crew. It was theory versus reality, and reality always wins.

Despite being confident in my previous experience, I'd never had an assistant director, let alone an assistant assistant director, casting director, line producer, and so on. I never had so many people to work with, and I was supposed to be the one who knew it all.

Right before we started shooting *Born Bad*, the partners at The Asylum asked me to a very nice lunch. Immediately, I assumed the worst and convinced myself they were taking me out to ease the blow of telling me I was fired, or the movie was off. I was so used to bad news that I couldn't imagine anything else.

I sat down at this fancy joint in Burbank, surrounded by the partners of The Asylum. As an actor, I had interacted with them over the years, but having them all together in one room was intimidating. I glanced at the expensive menu, looking for the right thing to order. Not the most expensive, but not the cheapest. I settled on the chicken, and after some small talk, David Rimawi kindly informed me that if I screwed up the movie in any way, I would be replaced. They were putting up a lot of money to make *Born Bad*, so fucking up wasn't an option. Yikes. I gulped and assured them I would do my absolute best and then ate my chicken.

Finding producers that believe in you enough to produce your story is hard. It's their money they're trusting you with, and without money, there is no movie. These relationships are the lifeblood of the industry, and I am grateful to The Asylum and every other producer who has supported me along my journey.

The sight of trailers and cube trucks on the first day of shooting was a satisfying moment. This was way different from shooting *And So They Die* or *Underground Lizard People* with minimal crew and definitely no trailers.

Born Bad was being shot on the then-new Red One camera, which I was very excited about. Red was a game changer: a studio-quality 4K digital cinema camera. I even posed for photos with the cameras on set to post to Facebook immediately.

Our main location was this big, beautiful house out in affluent Calabasas. We paid a premium to rent the place for the shoot, and since I was flying in from New York, I crashed at that house during production. I was told I wasn't allowed to, but I didn't want to pay for a hotel. I would wait until everyone left for the day and then sneak back in to pass out.

At night, I'd walk around by myself, stepping over cases of equipment and looking out over Calabasas, a world away from Long Island. I was really doing it this time. This was a real movie with a proper budget, and in the quiet, I was finally able to appreciate it.

My assistant director (AD) Glen Miller and director of photography (DP) Alex Yellen were veterans of moviemaking. The relationship between the director and these two roles is crucial. The AD runs the set and is in charge of departmental communications with the director, and the DP is in charge of the image—that is, what the movie actually looks like. These are the two people the director deals with most on set, usually way more than they deal with the actors. The AD, DP, and director are the three people that always need to know what exactly is going on and what should happen next.

The AD is also responsible for keeping the director on schedule. This can lead to conflict if you, the director, want to spend more time filming a scene than was originally accounted for. If the day is winding down and the AD says there's only time for one more shot, the director can keep insisting on more time. The AD will get pissed, but until a producer shuts you down for not wanting to pay overtime, you can technically keep going. The crew may hate you and will move slower the next day, but it can be done. That said, I learned the hard way not to repeat it in the future. You cannot expect the crew or anyone else to care about the movie you are directing as much as you do. The crew might care deeply about doing their job as best as possible, but that's different from caring about the overall movie or not caring about overtime.

When it came to developing the look of *Born Bad*, I still didn't know shit about lighting for a big crew. I was so used to just picking up my camera, setting a light or two, and shooting. On day one of *Born Bad*, I looked over to see guys carrying giant lights and silks for a shot and grew impatient. There were plenty of lights and stands already, more than enough—or at least that's what I thought. I called out impatiently, eager to start shooting.

The DP, Alex, calmly walked up to me and put me back in my place by telling me the shot was not ready and turned off the director's monitor. I huffed and puffed, thinking I knew better, but when it was finally set and Alex turned the monitor back on, it looked great. Humbled for a moment, I realized there was a huge difference between lighting an indie movie and lighting a feature film. I never again questioned Alex's lighting after that.

Holding on to the attitude you had as a one-man production team will not serve you on a proper movie set. I was so used to doing everything myself that I did not understand why all the departments needed to be involved in every shot or why people needed to know what was next. It didn't take long to see that communication protocol exists for a reason. Luckily, I adapted quickly, and as I learned to trust people more, things ran more smoothly.

Each day of the shoot, the producer, David Latt, would watch the dailies—raw footage from the previous day. After reviewing the dailies, David would email us his thoughts. Every director that's worked with The Asylum is familiar with Latt's notes. Latt is a filmmaking wizard and knows what works and what doesn't. If something looks bad, he is not afraid to call it out. For instance, I shot an early scene for *Born Bad* with an actor against a plain white wall, and when Latt saw that, he ripped me apart. He tore me up for not utilizing the location. There is no cheaper-looking shot than an actor standing in front of a white wall. He taught me the valuable lesson of putting the money on the screen. Never again did I shoot an actor flat against a white wall. In fact, the persistent fear of getting torn apart in an email with all the partners cc'd made me a better filmmaker. Even when I'm not directing an Asylum movie, I still sometimes expect an email full of Latt's notes.

For the climax of *Born Bad*, the angry mom played by Meredith Monroe needed to hit the bad guy, Michael Welch, with her car. The plan was to have the stunt performer roll heel over head across the car's roof to end the movie with a big action shot. We had a stunt driver, a body double to take the hit, a stunt coordinator, and a medic. The body double was decked out in all sorts of hidden pads, and I was convinced it was going to be the biggest shot I'd ever done.

Before I became a filmmaker, I had watched countless studio movies but few independent films, and the big studio blockbusters were always jam-packed with explosions and fast cars in every other scene. That's what I wanted to do for *Born Bad*. Film school did help me grow an appreciation for indie films, but I wanted to do big things, like what I saw in the movie theater.

Despite my vision and planning, this awesome stunt would not be how the movie ended. It turns out the car we had been using didn't have the right type of brakes or proper prefabrication to perform the hit, and the location was too small to do it the way I wanted. I was bummed. I had envisioned this awesome ending, but my lack of stunt experience got the better of me.

The best we could do was a side hit where the stunt double is "hit" but dives out of the way. I wasn't too thrilled. I kept thinking about Michael Bay spending a million dollars of his own money to blow something up in *Bad Boys* and how cool that was.

I had watched behind-the-scenes videos of how Michael Bay, Quentin Tarantino, and Peter Berg worked and seen their insistence on getting what they wanted. They took full command of their sets. Nobody likes being told no, but I didn't need to be reminded that I wasn't Michael Bay or making Michael Bay money. I was stuck with what the production would allow: it was the side hit or no hit.

The ending shot looked pretty cool and told the story, but I was still bummed we couldn't make it more visually spectacular. I had read about James Cameron's quest for spectacle and wanted to follow suit and go as big as possible. James Cameron is the type of director no studio says no to because he makes them billions of dollars. If he wants to sink the *Titanic* or create a different world, he can do it. I swore to myself at that moment, that's where I would be one day. I wanted to be the director nobody would say no to.

I was excited about finishing *Born Bad* and entering postproduction. I thought it could be something that elevated my career, and I would finally be on my way. I was so stoked that I booked a venue to host a party for when it premiered on TV. I invited my family and friends, and when my name popped up in the credits, people clapped. For a moment, I felt a little better about myself. Hollywood had chewed me up and spit me out, but I'd gone back for redemption.

When the movie did well, I figured I could use the buzz to attract a directing agent or manager and get more work. Confident, I reached out, boasting about my Lifetime movie credit. In return, I got crickets. No new text messages showed up on my phone. No emails from agents or managers or producers. Absolutely nothing had changed. Before long, it was back to shooting video, editing, and writing.

I'm still very proud of *Born Bad.* I heard it was the most-watched movie on Lifetime the summer it came out.

Tucked in the back seat directing Bonnie Dennison and Michael Welch in Born Bad.

Traced

After the sea of agents failed to come calling, I decided to write an expensive action script about an ex-race car driver forced to use his driving skill to rescue his kidnapped wife. The script, *Traced*, was different from my other "contained" scripts, which is a movie that can be "shot for a price" or low budget. *Traced* was my high-priced ticket to hitting the big time.

I was so serious about *Traced* that I paid for a coverage report, which is when you pay a professional reader to critique your script. If you're a screenwriter, I highly recommend getting coverage for any script before sending them out to your contacts. It's worth it. They will most likely shit all over your work and make suggestions that you hate, but as long as the service is legit, they're usually right. For *Traced*, I had coverage done five times and went through fourteen drafts. I was all in.

I submitted *Traced* to various screenwriting competitions and won the grand prize at the twenty-seventh WriteMovies contest. The prize was a couple grand and a nice luncheon in LA, where I was introduced to a few producers.

When you win a legit screenwriting contest, you think your script is the shit. I was bragging around town, confident I had the next big thing in my pocket. But no one I knew was in any position to make a movie with the budget *Traced* needed, so I had to hit the town and pitch the script to other industry executives.

I went to InkTip's pitchfest at the Marriott in Burbank. The only way to describe a pitchfest is it's like speed dating for screenwriters.

You only get five minutes to talk to a producer, agent, development executive, director, or whoever else.

I figured if I was going to book myself a plane ticket and spend money to get into this thing, I better give the pitchfest my all. I bought myself a nice button-down shirt, cut my mop of hair, and even shaved to look presentable.

I got there early because I wanted to pitch all the top companies I could. Unfortunately, I wasn't the only one who had the idea. Almost an hour before the Marriott's doors opened, the parking lot was packed with a line of economy cars waiting to get in. I watched a hundred aspiring screenwriters practice their pitches as they waited to enter the ballroom.

Despite feeling a little bit like cattle, I joined a line comprised mostly of other dudes in button-downs. As soon as the doors opened, the writers surged toward premiere companies like Lionsgate and the Creative Artists Agency. Everyone wanted to pitch the top folks, so I had to figure out the best way to maximize my time. There was no way I could get to everyone I wanted, so I shuffled my priorities and started with the less-busy options. In my very first pitch, I gave an exciting plot synopsis of *Traced* to a young executive in a much nicer button-down shirt and glasses.

At the end, he chimed in and asked, "What's the budget?"

I had no idea but said 20 million because I saw it on the coverage report I paid for.

He told me he was happy to read *Traced*, but he produced movies for 1 million, not 20 million. He said that if I could attach an A-list actor to it, he could then get the money, even implying it would be easy. It was at that point I realized I didn't really know how moviemaking worked, but I was happy to be there learning.

The other attendees were cool creatives who were happy to share advice. The people being pitched to mostly worked in development for a production company or were representatives looking for new clients. It was a mix of both top and junior executives, some of them very junior, so there was a lot of information going around.

Soon I found myself with time for one only more pitch. I jumped in an empty line without knowing anything about the company and found myself across the table from an older lady. Halfway through my pitch, she cut me off and asked if my movie was animated. Surprised, I looked down to see other pitches filled with cartoon sketches. Turns out I was selling an action script to a company looking for animated television series. Regardless, I still told her "It could be animated!" She just shook her head and said politely, "This wouldn't work for us. Thanks." Embarrassing.

Other than my last-minute faux pas, I met a lot of great people, some of whom I still am in contact with today. The experience was definitely worth the price of admission. I left with a gang of business cards and a fair amount of people interested in reading *Traced*, just not the animation company.

After I got home, I sent my script out to anyone and everyone who expressed a degree of interest. A few calls and emails came in over the weeks, and I was pleased to see that producers were interested in making the movie. In fact, several legit companies liked the script. I spent time going back and forth with producers until I was close to landing a deal with a very respectable company that was prepared to shell out millions to make *Traced*. Officially, we were "in talks." The time from the pitchfest to getting close to an actual deal took almost a year, but it all would be worth it if it worked out. But just as it was looking like a sure thing, everything changed.

My phone rings one day, and the voice on the other line says, "Did you see the trailer for *Getaway*?" I hadn't, so I went online to see it, and my jaw dropped. *Traced* followed the story of an ex-race car driver using his skills to rescue his kidnapped wife, and the trailer for *Getaway* was about, you guessed it, an ex-race car driver having to use his driving skills to rescue his kidnapped wife. I couldn't believe it. Did somebody steal my script? I needed to get ahold of the *Getaway* script to find out for myself. Luckily, I knew a few people who worked in development, and I was able to get a copy and dove in. The more I read, the more it felt like I was reading an alternate version of my own script. The plots were too similar. The worst part about it was the producer who was interested in making *Traced* suddenly ghosted me.

I did a lot of research into who made *Getaway* and compared it to the people I pitched *Traced* to. I found a connection between one of the people I spoke with in Santa Monica and a producer responsible for *Getaway*. Facebook friends, mutual connections. I thought I had them dead to rights.

I called an intellectual property lawyer to see what my options were. After a consultation call, the lawyer recommended I create a side-by-side document to prove where my script and *Getaway* were similar. So I went to work creating a long and detailed comparison. I set my script on one side of the page and *Getaway* on the other to show that someone had read and retooled it. There was too much coincidence.

I sent my thoughtful, lengthy document to the intellectual property attorney, who was impressed with my work. He agreed I had a case but warned that with a major company being involved in *Getaway,* a lawsuit would be an expensive uphill battle. After some huffing and puffing, I realized I didn't have the money to pursue it.

I gave up on *Traced.* Later, when I watched *Getaway,* I kept thinking the movie would have been better if they'd just used my script. However, for legal reasons, I will say it's possible that someone had the same idea for a movie at the same time I did. Maybe nobody stole anything. I will never know, and it doesn't really matter anymore. Maybe one day *Traced* will get produced for real.

Getaway felt like a major bump in the road for me. I had won a contest and made real traction with my action script, only to have it all come screeching to a halt. It was back to square one, to starting all over again. I did the only thing I could do: I went back to the drawing board. Fueled by anger, I decided to write another "big" script that I could attach myself to as director. I put on Rage Against the Machine and was caught by a lyric at the end of "Man without a Face." Zack de la Rocha screams out the word *reaction.* In that moment, I knew I too had to react.

So I started work on *Reactor,* a movie about one man against the world, taking out the bad guys. Art can be aspirational, I guess.

Bikini Spring Break (2011)

B efore *Born Bad* came out, I thought I was going to be the next Scorsese because I had a movie on TV. Funny how the brain always thinks there's a magic ticket inside every chocolate bar. I was proud of my work, but that didn't mean the phone rang because of all the major studios contacting me. Instead, it rang because a doctor in Long Island wanted a video. I made the doctor the video.

After realizing that having a TV movie under my belt wasn't going to get the top agency in town to sign me, reality set in. I went about making videos for cash and writing in my spare time. I knew I wanted to make movies and not videos, but the universe didn't seem to give a fuck. As more time passed after *Born Bad*, my hopes of directing more movies began to fade.

"Fuck it," I said. I would just be the Long Island video guy. Maybe I could hire an editor and grow my one-man video business into a little company. So much work was already coming in that I had to turn down jobs, so expanding was a reasonable plan.

Then my phone rang, and this time it wasn't a local business wanting a video. The call was from David Latt, partner and head of production at The Asylum. I answered, happy to receive a call from Hollywood while stuck in my cramped bedroom in my dad's apartment in Long Island.

David mentioned an upcoming project The Asylum was doing called *Bikini Spring Break*, a sexy comedy with buyers already lined up and a delivery date set. They had no script and no director, but they had a short outline for it. He asked me if it was something I would be interested in writing and directing.

The Asylum has a genius business model. Every movie they make is presold to direct buyers. They found the magic trick to movie distribution and production and operate like a full-on movie studio. Sometimes they produce as many as thirty new movies a year.

Of course, I wanted to write and direct *Bikini Spring Break*. I was a twenty-eight-year-old guy being asked to write and direct a movie with a bunch of attractive actresses. Besides, being back in LA seemed like a great escape from my mundane life making videos in Long Fucking Island.

The instructions were to write an outline for a script with sexy, fun humor and a lot of nudity.

I watched a bunch of sexy comedies and even some romantic ones to try and follow the brief. I didn't want to outright copy other people's work, but I tried to capture the same light-hearted tone as best I could. Unfortunately, I struggled to make anything interesting without crazy shit happening.

The core of the story is about a group of girls whose car breaks down en route to a band competition, so they have to make money to get there on time. However, I wrote an outline that started light but changed when the girls started doing drugs and hooking up with each other.

Stories need conflict to be interesting. Every time I wrote a scene without conflict, it felt boring. I put a lot of time into my drafts to rework those scenes, but no matter what I did, the script always turned out edgy. Too edgy. Eventually I had to send something in, so I sent what I had. It was not received well. One remark simply stated, "Not fun and cute."

I thought maybe I just wasn't a funny guy, but the truth was I had never written a comedy before. There was always humor in my scripts, but a straight comedy was a completely different animal, never mind a sexy comedy. At the time, I wasn't aware of the distinction between genres, and everyone suffered for it. Despite the studio partners' concerns, I assured them the full script would be more in line with the tone they were after, and after some begging and pleading, they agreed to let me take another crack at it.

I decided I should not just watch other sexy comedies but actually read their scripts. Maybe that would help the tone resonate in my head. Every day for the next week, I read comedy scripts like *American Pie* and *Groundhog Day*, two of my all-time favorites. This exercise helped, but when I went to create an original story, it kept leaning dark.

I gave it my best shot. I hunkered down and wrote day in and day out. By the end of my last writing session, I thought the script was pretty good. It was unique and edgy, kind of like what you'd see at an indie festival. Unfortunately that was exactly what the producers didn't want. I still hadn't cracked the comedy code. The script was still not fun or cute. They told me very clearly it wasn't working for them.

I was in trouble. If they didn't like the script, there was a chance they wouldn't make the movie or, worse, make the movie without me. I panicked, sure I had just fucked up everything. Surprisingly, they didn't cut me loose. Instead, they gave my draft to another writer, Naomi Selfman. And Naomi "got" it. She rewrote *Bikini*

Spring Break, keeping my characters and some of the skeleton of my story. She made it exactly what the producers wanted: fun and cute, with Jell-O wrestling and a wet T-shirt contest.

It's weird to read a rewritten version of a script you wrote. Your brain tries to process it as something you recognize, but it's different. At first, my mind rejected the rewrite—it could not comprehend all the changes! My work, torn apart and rearranged? How could she? But it was better. It had silly jokes, and the characters were quirky. It was what it should have been, what it needed to be. She more than deserved the shared "written by" credit.

With a script locked down, we were off to preproduction land. We needed locations, a supporting cast, and a star name. We managed to snag Robert Carradine from *Revenge of the Nerds*, and again I was excited to be directing a big star.

Finding good locations was harder. We spent days looking at schools and strip clubs and scouting bars with mechanical bulls. There were all sorts of unusual location challenges. The more specific the location, the harder it was to find.

Although location scouting can be exhausting, it's also exciting. You're given the power to stop and rearrange a live location at your whim or to traipse around a workspace that you'd normally not have access to. Those moments are part of why I enjoy being a filmmaker and supporting the creation of escapism.

It felt great to be back in the swing of making a movie rather than a piddly video. I was soaking it all in because I knew I'd be heading back to Long Island soon enough.

When it came time to audition, thousands of girls submitted for the fully clothed roles, but filling the ones that required nudity was a bit more challenging. After we narrowed down our selections, it was time to see what they looked like nude to make sure everything would look good on camera. At the same time, I didn't want to be the creepy guy asking a girl to take her top off in an audition room, so I met with my producers.

In the end, we had a female casting assistant conduct nude tests in a private room where the footage would only be shown to me and the producers. It feels shallow, but this was a sexy comedy, so it was important that the girls looked great. That said, even writing about this makes me a tad uneasy, but that is the movie business.

In Los Angeles, gorgeous, talented girls weren't hard to come by, but our biggest hurdle was a male actor. One point in the script called for a character to moon another as the punchline to a big joke for a scene. The move was in the approved script, but on the day of the shoot, the actor suddenly didn't want to do it. I was stressed. If it was in the approved script, I needed to shoot it. If I didn't shoot it, all sorts of bad things could happen, like getting fired. If I didn't get the shot, the entire joke wouldn't work, and the movie would suffer.

I also worried that without getting the shot, I would be seen as a weak director who couldn't get his actors to fulfill the vision. The actor had read the script and signed on to do the bit, so why would he suddenly back out? I didn't know what to do. I thought about asking the producers if it would be okay to skip the bit, but even calling and asking felt weak.

I was stuck between a rock and a hard place. While I had empathy for the actor—I certainly wouldn't want to show my privates—it was the role he signed up for, and we needed the shot.

As respectfully as I could, I insisted we do the scene. Despite the cutting look he shot me, the actor complied. It was uncomfortable having to assert myself, but at the end of the day, I was proud to have maintained the integrity of the script and delivered the footage to the producers. The Asylum had given me a chance, and I had failed to deliver a solid script. I wouldn't fail to deliver *Bikini Spring Break* as intended. I was and will be forever indebted to them for all the opportunities and second chances. This one was no different.

After wrapping, I worked with the editor, sound designer, and colorist to get *Bikini Spring Break* in solid shape. It turned out to be a fun and cute movie, and it even aired on Showtime. That made for a good Facebook post, but that was it. It was time to go back to reality.

With the main cast of Bikini Spring Break.

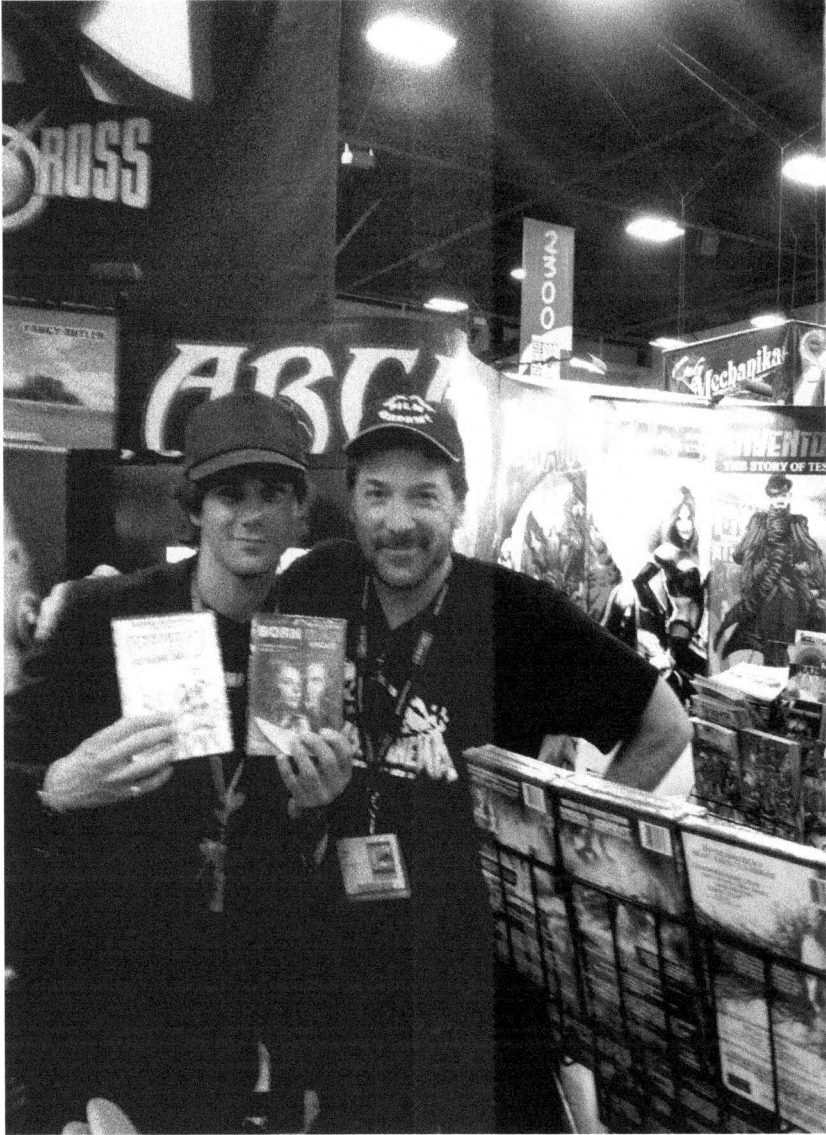

With David Latt at Comic-Con, promoting Bikini Spring Break.

The Good, the Bad, and the Ugly

It was the same cycle as before. I got excited to direct a movie and live the creative life, and then was right back in New York. My phone went from ringing with exciting calls from the crew and producers to clients wanting me to make additional revisions to their videos.

It was like I was living two different lives. Sometimes I would go to Hollywood and do cool stuff, but the majority of the time I was miserable, working at home in the chill of Long Island. Some of the video work I did was fun, and some of the people I met were great to work with, but I still wanted to make movies. I had thought I was gaining traction, but reality deflates all hopes and dreams with time. Hollywood was not calling, only people in Long Island who wanted me to make videos. There was no crew and definitely no star names. All of the editing, music, and titles fell to me. I was getting burned out.

My only projects outside of work were the various scripts I was working on. Ping-ponging between video editing and screenwriting became my routine, which is not a healthy lifestyle ergonomically speaking. I was staring at a screen all day and then typing at night. By the time I went to bed, my hands would be cramped, and my eyes would be aching.

Months later, my face was buried in Adobe Premiere as I edited footage from a celebrity golf event. Then my phone lit up. David Latt is not the type of person who calls for no reason.

Snapping out of my funk, I picked up, and he told me about another upcoming project The Asylum was going to produce, a horror movie called *Hold Your Breath*. Unlike previous projects, this one would be released in theaters, and they already had a script. He asked me if I was interested in directing. I didn't need long to think. There I was in my pajamas, potato chip bags and pizza boxes scattered around my workstation. Clearly a change of scenery was in order. Needless to say, I agreed.

This new prospect was reinvigorating. I thought about my life in New York and what to do next. Suddenly it occurred to me: I needed to give up my video business and move back to LA and try my luck one last time. There was no way I could stay in New York any longer. I couldn't keep shooting and editing videos. I needed to be back west if I wanted a career as a movie director. I needed it for my own sanity.

It was traumatizing leaving LA the first time, but I had higher hopes for my second attempt. Despite leaving my business, I still brought all my film and editing equipment. If I wasn't making movies out west, I could at least try and find work making videos for some cash. As much as I hated editing, I was glad I knew how to do it.

Those first six years in LA were my first tour of duty. Now it was time to head back for round two. This time I would be focused on directing and writing, not acting.

I had struggled to accept that I was officially moving on from my acting pursuits. Performing was a joy, but now I wouldn't have to race to get new headshots. I would be the movie director guy instead. It felt more comfortable. When I first moved to LA to act, it took me years to feel confident enough to tell strangers I was an actor. Now things were a bit different, and having a college degree in film made me feel confident about presenting as a director.

But my anxiety over whether or not to give up my video business and move back to LA crippled me. Could I really afford to leave everything behind? My finances weren't great, and Los Angeles is the perfect place to make that kind of situation worse. In the end, I did it. I powered through my mental anguish and booked a flight to LA without finding a place to stay. I called some contacts and found a room available with a friend of a friend at a house in the Hollywood Hills. It was perfect, I thought.

I didn't think too much about what could go wrong with living with this guy. When I showed up, I was already stressing about the upcoming movie and not in the best place mentally. My new roommate, Randy, found this hysterical and made a point to be hypercritical of me for giving up my business and how I handled personal matters. Randy was the type of guy who laughs when someone hurts themselves. He was on me like a vulture.

With the house being up in the Hollywood Hills, you'd think it would have been cool as shit. The Hills are famous because of all the writers, directors, and actors living there who have created amazing works, but my experience was the polar opposite. It was misery with a million-dollar view.

Randy had a habit of waking up at ungodly hours to make hostile investment calls, most of which ended in him leaving long, scathing voicemails. He also didn't believe in closing the door when he used the bathroom, so I got to see him taking a shit, which only made him laugh. It wasn't a normal laugh either; it had this whiney cackle to it like nails on a chalkboard. I told myself it was a temporary arrangement, and the price was much better than a hotel.

I was doing everything I could to stay focused on *Hold Your Breath*, but my crippling anxiety was weighing me down. Past clients were calling and asking for videos, and one by one, I told them I was shutting down shop. Each lost opportunity raised the pressure I was under. The business I had spent so long and worked so hard to build up was vanishing before my sad eyes.

Racked with anxiety, I stopped being able to sleep. I had dealt with insomnia before, but this was different. The sleeping pills I was taking didn't even help, and my mind filled with a new level of fog. I had started prep on *Hold Your Breath* but was so sleep deprived, I could barely manage the location scouting or casting. Even my basic communication was suffering. I could barely eat food consistently, let alone drive a car or direct a movie. I was so mad at myself for not being able to sleep, and that frustration made it even worse. Lying in bed and not being able to sleep is the worst pain I've ever experienced. It sucks the first night, the second is god-awful, and the third is hellacious. It wasn't long before I was on the brink of insanity.

While location scouting for *Hold Your Breath*, we looked at a beautiful thirty-acre movie ranch in Santa Clarita. Movie ranches are plots of land with all sorts of standing sets on them. It had a church, gas station, pond, house, cabins, shacks, and all manner of woods and cliffs. On one part of the movie ranch, the foliage was planted to look like a Vietnam War–era jungle, while another was designed to look like the Middle East; the place was packed with different environments.

We rolled up—the line producer, AD, cinematographer, and I—in search of woods that we could build a cemetery in. I looked strung out, I hadn't slept a minute all week, and as I walked through the woods, the changing foliage caught me off guard. Before I knew it, I had wandered off by myself and gotten lost. I had never been there before and had no cell service to call for help. I looked around, too embarrassed to call out for the others. I just laughed. I had wanted to escape, right? Well there I was, so "free" I was lost. I sat down against a tree for a moment and slapped myself across the face to try to rejoin reality.

After twenty minutes of trekking through a marsh, I finally saw the parking lot. The giant cross on the church set stared down at me like a sign from above. God was telling me I needed some fucking sleep. But first, I needed to find the others, which was easy after I heard someone yell, "Yo! Where the hell did you go?"

The *Hold Your Breath* production had me working with a new AD and cinematographer, and these guys were sharp. I had *Born Bad* and *Bikini Spring Break* under my belt, but as sleep deprived as I was, all that experience was worthless. Every single decision I made was impaired by my mental state, even when we started filming. My communication with the actors suffered, and my answers to simple questions were fumbling and stumbling mumbling.

Usually, when I'm asked a question on set, I answer right away as efficiently and effectively as possible. Some days I answer a thousand questions: "The art department needs to know if you like the painting on the wall. Wardrobe needs approval on a shirt." Directing involves making rapid-fire decisions, so if you're sleep deprived, you're fucked.

Thanks to my compromised mental state, I did not get on too well with the cinematographer and AD. To be fair to them, it's hard to respect a director who takes ten minutes to answer a simple question like where a camera should go.

It felt like I was trapped inside a worse, weaker version of myself. I wanted so badly to jump out of my skin—to be energized and take control. But I couldn't. My arms were heavy, and it was damn near impossible to keep my eyeballs open. With my garbled speech—I didn't have the energy to properly enunciate—directing the actors became even more of a challenge, and when they had questions, it was a hundred times more difficult to answer. I would go on rants and overthink things, which slowed us down further. The AD, whose job it is to keep the show on schedule, was not too keen on this. He would huff and puff and throw his purple binder onto the dirt in protest.

Each night, I would slink onto my mattress on the floor of this great house in the Hollywood Hills, while my roommate shouted at the television. It would only be after complaining about me having a messy room for an hour that he would eventually leave me alone each night. I would lay there, close my eyes, and pray for sleep that wouldn't come.

I would periodically check the time on my phone: 2:48 a.m. would become 3:57 a.m., then 5:04 a.m., and the ink-black sky would slowly lighten to dark and then light blue. Every dawn, I wondered if there was something terribly wrong with me. I would drive to the set in a haze, weaving across the highway as the sleeping pills still clouded my mind. Some mornings, I would fall into desperation and swallow a second drug cocktail at 3:00 a.m., hoping to fall asleep but only feeling like I slammed four shots of tequila. When the alarm sounded, my frail body would come to, and I'd stumble to my rental car to get to the set. I had work to do, I had a movie to direct, and I refused to be a no-show.

After a few days of acting like a bumbling idiot, I found myself eating lunch alone and feeling helpless. I couldn't hold a coherent conversation, and nobody wanted anything to do with me. It felt like the crew had turned against me. I'd see people looking my way and whispering under their breath. Some of that was surely exaggerated by my delusional mind, but it was also very real. People likely wondered how the hell I landed the job, and they would've been right to question it. I had no business being there in that condition. I should've been on a stretcher with fluids being pumped into me so I could get my brain scanned.

This was another SAG movie, and I was supposed to be captain of the ship, directing the stars. We had cast Katrina Bowden, who was hot off *30 Rock*, and Randy Wayne from *Dukes of Hazzard*. I should've been ecstatic, but I was a mess. The actors struggled to work with my indecisiveness, and I couldn't blame them. Actors want to land on set with a director who knows their shit and can command a movie like a boss. That's usually how I rolled. I was on point—sharp—but after not sleeping for two weeks, I was about as dull as a rusted butter knife.

Despite the mental fog, I still pushed hard to make sure the movie didn't suck. The script included some visual effects (VFX), and I was just beginning to understand how to shoot for them. It's hard to imagine things that aren't there, let alone get people to react realistically to those imaginary things. It takes an articulate imagination and effective communication skills to shoot scenes with a lot of VFX, and my being exhausted didn't help.

I got notes from David Latt, and they were not glowing. The hardest one to take simply said, "I know you can do better." He went on to critique my static blocking and basic shots. He saw no artistry in my work: "It's crafting at best." He wasn't wrong. The shots so far weren't my best work, and his criticism further fueled my desire to make the movie better. I stayed up all night planning the shots for the next several days, drafting drawings, and writing detailed shot lists. I figured if I concocted some cool camera moves, it would make up for my otherwise bland direction.

Once on set the next day, I tried to explain my new creative vision, and the crew looked at me like I was speaking Klingon. The diagrams I spent so long on made no sense—or at least I could not explain them with enough conviction. I was too tired. The actors sensed my weakness and pushed back until I was ready to jump off a cliff. No matter what I tried, I kept coming up short. In hindsight, the whole process was a valuable lesson in making sure you are in a good mental state before taking on a massive responsibility. At the time, however, it didn't feel like that. Most people think I'm lying when I say I didn't get a wink of sleep for eighteen days, but it's the truth. I'll never know how my body didn't shut down and how I didn't go crazy, but I was close.

Despite feeling like shit, what felt worse was letting David Latt and The Asylum team down. They all believed in me. They could've called a hundred different directors for *Hold Your Breath*, but they chose me. That meant I had to power through. I had to see that the movie got done, no matter what shape I was in. I will always feel bad for not doing better in those early days, for allowing myself to be compromised.

When the shoot was done, I was ready to sleep for a month, but my roommate didn't allow that. I would have to wait until the editing process was done.

To my surprise during postproduction, the movie was shaping up much better than expected. I thought it would watch like a trashy student film, yet the story worked, the shots looked good, and the acting was solid. Despite the fear that I had destroyed my career, the final cut wasn't all bad. The movie gods had not quite smiled on me, but thankfully they had smirked. It didn't matter to me if The Asylum partners liked my previous movies because you're only as good as the last movie you made. *Hold Your Breath* wasn't my best work, but it did work, so I could breathe a sigh of relief.

As the editing wrapped, I saw David Latt roller-skating around the poster-filled hallways of The Asylum office, as he usually did. He would pop his head into the editing bays to check on the various films being cut together and sometimes throw jabs at the shots, like commenting that some of our blocking looked "stagey." That one stung.

A couple of weeks later, I was sitting next to the editor when I heard my name called. I raced over to the executive office shared by David Latt, David Rimawi, and Paul Bales. Three big chairs sat there surrounded by awards, plaques, and movie posters while phone calls continued in full swing. Sitting across from the three of them can be a bit intimidating. Not only did they hold my future, but all three are ultraquick-witted, and any weakness will instantly be called out. I feared the worst.

Maybe they summoned me to tell me I fucked up the movie and was done. I mean, I knew the partners were all watching the various stages of rough cuts. Maybe they were there to collectively tell me I should give up my directing hopes and be a production assistant. Yeah, they definitely were going to rip into me.

12/12/12 (2012)

Thankfully I wasn't called into the executive offices to be told I suck. Instead, the partners had called me in to talk about another new project, a movie called *12/12/12*, set to release only a few months away on, you guessed it, *12/12/12*. According to them, they needed a script yesterday, and the shooting needed to start two weeks out. Then they asked me a question I was happy to answer: "Are you up for the challenge?"

Of course I was! I was sure they were about to complain about *Hold Your Breath*, and instead I got offered another movie to write and direct. I leaped at the opportunity, determined to not make the same mistakes I did on *Hold Your Breath*.

As I sat in bumper-to-bumper traffic in Burbank, the bright, smog-filtered winter sun beaming down, I realized I had done the unthinkable. Round 2 in LA would not be cut short by failure, not today. I had powered through the worst experience of my life, and it hadn't been for nothing. I felt blessed to have the opportunity to redeem myself. This time I would make sure I got sleep, so I went home and had a stern word with my roommate.

I told him I had a movie to write and needed to focus. His response: "You're more than welcome to find other living arrangements." I really wanted to leave, but with a script to write in less than a week, there was no time to apartment shop. So I did the next best thing and put on some headphones, cranked up my angsty nineties playlist, and got to work.

My first order of business was to write an outline for a horror movie about December 12—more specifically, a horror movie about an evil baby born on December 12. Despite the outrageousness, I took the process seriously. If I'm tasked with making a movie about an evil baby, well, I'm going to make the best movie about an evil baby I can.

I struggled with the outline. My first draft was too dramatic, involving a love story that results in a demonic baby. It was something, but it wasn't really horror. The Asylum hated it, so I trashed the draft and started over. I racked my brain for story options. Maybe the baby has mind powers? Could it be that it's not a baby but the devil in disguise? My mind was spinning out of control, so I sent David Latt a few versions of a one-pager and got an email back saying, "This isn't working for us." I must've been visibly distressed because my roommate saw this as an opportunity to remind me I was an idiot for thinking I might succeed in the industry.

Then The Asylum told me if I couldn't crack the script, they would find someone else. I had to write better! I was so anxious, the sleep demons returned and brought the nightly rumination with them. The more my roommate sensed I was struggling, the more he antagonized me, and the worse my sleep became. It was a vicious cycle.

I found myself thinking back to providing video services in Long Island and how that was going to be my life forever. Maybe I couldn't craft an interesting story about a killer baby who turns out to be the devil. It didn't matter that I had graduated film school cum fucking laude. I was just some hack writer who couldn't handle an outline.

Questioning yourself can take you to deep, painful places, and this was no different. Was I a good writer, I wondered? If I was, why couldn't I do this?

Once again, Micho Rutare from The Asylum's development department came to the rescue. I had been sending all sorts of new pitches for completely different storylines, all of which missed the mark. In the midst of this, Micho sent a quick email that saved me. He broke down my fumbling outlines and gave me concise bullet points that guided me in the right direction.

I took Micho's advice, and it was exactly what the story needed. It wasn't long before I banged out a new outline, and this one was different: this one was right. Everything about it worked better. A day later, I got the green light via email. "We approve the outline. Write the script."

The second I read that, I was right back to my laptop, ready to hammer out the script. Headphones on, I tuned out the world and my crazy roommate and got down to business.

I had less than a week to deliver a first draft. Usually writers spend months, even years writing and rewriting a script, but I had to get something film ready in less than a week. I drank quite a few Red Bulls in the name of progress.

That week was a blur until I typed "The End." I reread the script before sending it in and thought it turned out pretty well. After all, I had used the bullet points Micho had given me as a roadmap. Despite the tight timeline, I believed a good script can be written in a week. *Rocky* was written in just three and a half days. *12/12/12* is no *Rocky*—I'm just saying it's possible. And to my delight, The Asylum liked my submission, and the script was approved.

We brought in veteran Asylum DP Ben Demaree, while Max Elfeldt and Mike Meilander came on as line producers, and John Mehrer joined as my second AD. These guys were experienced, and the movie was already feeling a lot stronger than *Hold Your Breath*. I was sleeping, focused, and getting on well with people. I was not going to fuck this one up!

It's hard to say why I was so messed up on the *Hold Your Breath* shoot but fine on *12/12/12*. I think the process of giving up my video business, moving to LA, and coping with that while handling a crazy roommate just pushed me over. By the time *12/12/12* was underway, I wasn't getting calls from Long Island and watching my business disappear in front of my face. Before, I was suffering from loss. Now I had nothing to lose. Without as many anxieties holding me back, I was able to deal with my crazy roommate more effectively.

Late one day of casting, I was sitting in a room with a casting assistant after seeing a bunch of actresses trying to score the lead. While some of them were okay, none of them was our star. Just as hope was waning, in walks Sara Malakul Lane, a beautiful half-Thai, half-Caucasian actress. Sara crushed the audition and gave a fantastic performance, even summoning tears on the spot. Never before had I been so blown away by an audition. I knew I wanted her right away, and everyone else agreed.

When it came time to start filming, I was eager to flex my skills. Given the movie's supernatural undertone, I was pulling different shots than I normally would. I used canted, unconventional angles for otherwise conventional coverage. I wanted the movie to feel different and give the viewer a sense of unease.

One scene involved my friend, a talented actor named Jon Kondelick, who had unfortunately lost several fingers during a previous movie. I spoke with him about incorporating his unique hand into the film as though the evil baby had done it. I thought it would make for an edgy and interesting scene, and I was right. Luckily, he was down to play ball and gave a fantastic performance that culminated in his character's suicide by gunshot, the blood splattering over Sara. It was a powerful, memorable scene, and I thanked Jon for his courage and talent.

Everything was smooth sailing until it came time to shoot some of the truly crazy shit I wrote.

Since we were making a movie about a baby, I saw the opportunity to film an epic scene where we see the baby birthed before it turns violent and kills the doctors and nurses. I really wanted to push the limits, so I bought a Sasha Grey silicone vagina from a sex shop as a prop piece. Showing up to set with a plastic vagina was a bit much, but when we covered it in blood and goop and filmed the baby's head popping out of it, the shot was gnarly. It definitely gets a reaction when people see it. Getting a reaction from an audience, even if it's to gross them out, is better than no reaction at all. At least that's what I thought at the time.

The final cut had the demon baby bite people, make them commit suicide, and push people off cliffs. There was no moral to the story. The baby killed everyone and lived.

DP Ben Demaree, AC Jake Humbert, Steadicam operator Luke Rocheleau, and myself on 12/12/12.

Atlantic Rim (2013)

Despite working fairly consistently as a director, I was doing some work on the side again: shooting videos, editing actor demo reels, anything I could do to make money. LA is the city of twenty-dollar drinks, so I needed the extra cash.

Sara and I began dating after we wrapped *12/12/12*, and it was nice being with someone in the same industry. She was career focused, doing commercials, booking lead roles in movies, and modeling on the cover of magazines like *Maxim, Playboy,* and *FHM.* It was nice to have someone who got it and could be supportive. The movie business isn't for the faint of heart, so the more support you can get, the better. Film careers are rife with close calls, and it's good to have someone to lean on when a job disappears or is given to someone else.

Although making videos was keeping me afloat, the only way I was going to survive was if I continued directing. I didn't want to get sucked back into making videos full time. I was making just enough to get by, but I wanted more. I had ambition.

It felt like I hit a plateau, so I was looking for ways to advance my career. I had been watching movies nonstop, but now it was time to learn who the players were. My thirst for knowledge was renewed; I wanted to know the important producers, agents, managers, distributors, and directors. I needed to expand my network.

Reading trade publications became a religious habit. I devoured *The Hollywood Reporter* and *Deadline,* then read up on production companies to see who worked where and who was casting or producing what. I trolled IMDb and LinkedIn and even reached out to a few high-level folks (who never got back to me).

Although reading through IMDb is a good way to kill a few hours, it's not the same as making movies. Just because I read about the big Hollywood action didn't mean I was suddenly going to be in the thick of it. It was time to get back to work.

Fresh off a confidence boost from *12/12/12,* I drove to Burbank and popped my head into The Asylum's executive office to look for another job.

It's a competitive field; for every Asylum movie made, there are many directors wanting the job. I've seen countless directors walk in and drop off their demo reels. There's always some kid fresh out of film school looking to shoot their shot.

It felt good to have a close relationship with The Asylum after being so used to fighting for roles and hustling to get a job. It hadn't been long since I had been the guy dropping off headshots and scripts, and being able to walk into the offices without a set meeting was a big step up.

When I nudged The Asylum, they told me about an upcoming mockbuster, sometimes called a studio tie-in movie. A mockbuster is a movie that's made when a major blockbuster comes out. For example, when something *Transformers* released, The Asylum made another movie about giant robots called *Transmorphers,* capitalizing on the hype.

Speaking of giant robots, the mockbuster they were prepping was an action movie called *Atlantic Rim.* Not to be confused with *Pacific Rim,* which is about robots versus kaiju, *Atlantic Rim* is about sea creatures versus robots.

I think The Asylum's model of making mockbusters is brilliant. It means that they have a major studio pumping hundreds of millions of dollars into marketing a movie about giant robots, which makes people interested in watching any movie about giant robots. The Asylum rides the wave to catch the trend and profit. The reality of this industry is that if you can find any way to succeed, you've won. Everybody has to find their own path, and The Asylum was smart enough to carve out a niche for themselves and reap the rewards. I was just happy to be along for the ride. Little did I know, that ride was about to get a lot cooler . . .

Before I hopped on an airplane from California to Florida to direct *Atlantic Rim*, producers informed me that *GQ Magazine* would be doing an article on The Asylum and sending a reporter to Florida with us for the shoot. *Atlantic Rim* and photos of me directing would be featured in a seven-page article in the August 2013 *GQ* hardcover issue. The great Bryan Cranston was even slated to be on the cover. Like I said, way cooler.

Academy Award winner Graham Greene was also joining the movie along with Treach from superstar rap group Naughty by Nature. I would also be reuniting with *Born Bad* and *Baywatch* star David Chokachi. When I told the cast *GQ* would be down there with us, the excitement grew. Things were looking up.

When we landed in Pensacola, we hit the ground running. After getting settled in, we met up with a local coordinator who showed us around this suburban beach town and took us to review a navy base with huge production value. There were billions of dollars' worth of state-of-the-art aircraft armed with missiles while Hummers drove all around us. You couldn't find a bad angle to photograph the location, and we were told we'd have full run of the place. I was thrilled. Being allowed to film at a real military base was an incredible gift that would make the movie feel huge. Even the *GQ* reporter was impressed.

With the navy base secured, I shifted my focus to the other key component of the movie: the giant robot. I was adamant we use a practical robot suit for authenticity. Truth was, I still wasn't totally confident in my ability to direct with VFX in mind, so I thought it would be better to avoid them altogether. I convinced the producers to shell out a bunch of money to hire a custom costume maker. Now that we were going practical, I got to work sketching out ways to incorporate the robot suit and make it look bigger with forced perspective. Forced perspective is an old movie trick involving putting a smaller object close to the camera and a bigger object farther away to make the smaller object look huge. I thought I'd be crafty enough to pull it off.

A week later, a bunch of cardboard boxes showed up at the hotel. To our surprise—and my horror— it was the robot suit. And it wasn't great. The more parts we pulled out, the more it looked like someone went to Home Depot, grabbed a bunch of tubes, plywood, and glue, and spray-painted the whole thing metallic silver. At best, it looked straight out of a 1980s DIY home video. I was less than thrilled, but I was still imagining ways to make it work. Maybe we'd shoot it backlit at night or blast smoke everywhere to hide the suit as much as possible. With enough movie magic, I thought, no one would notice the cheapness.

Before we started shooting, the producer, David Latt, wanted to see some test footage of the robot suit in action. I figured the robot suit should be worn by a big, strong guy since the robot was supposed to be big and badass, so we called over one of the bigger crew members.

The production assistant (PA) was a bit above six feet, and as we put the suit on him, we realized he was way too big. Not a good sign. Going the opposite direction, we pulled the smallest person on the crew—a woman about five-foot-two—to try it out. The suit fit her, but barely. We had to squeeze her in, and the end result looked ridiculous. Nonetheless, we needed test footage, and some part of my brain still thought I could get something usable with enough smoke and mirrors. We set up a few different camera angles on the poor PA, who could barely walk in the clunky suit. She was supposed to be acting like she was fighting sea creatures, but it was more like she was swatting lazy flies. It was bad. There is no kinder word for it.

When David Latt saw the footage, he told us in no uncertain terms, "Do not use the suit!" So much for practical effects.

Knowing that every shot of the robot would now have to be computer generated, I had a chat with the head of The Asylum's VFX team, Joe Lawson. I grilled him about how to frame my shots for the giant robot, what to do, and what to avoid. He taught me a lot, including that I needed to be meticulous when framing for the VFX because if it wasn't shot right, I would create a lot of extra work for him, like rotoscoping things out. Rotoscoping is a time-consuming task of isolating something like a moving person and removing the background frame by hand. This happens when you don't shoot for VFX properly. It was clear that if I did that, the entire VFX team would hate my guts.

Joe advised me to shoot enough footage that didn't rely on VFX to make a watchable cut of the movie without effects. It was good advice because doing so forced me to get creative with the storytelling.

With locations locked and our robot issue sorted, things were progressing nicely. At least until the phone rang with bad news. Two days out from starting to film, we got an emergency call from one of the producers. Apparently an official from the Pentagon read the *Atlantic Rim* script and said there was no way we could film at an actual navy base. No further explanation was given. That meant all of the scenes at the navy base, which was 90 percent of the movie, were now without a location. I went into panic mode. I was so stoked we were going to be shooting at the base that I felt as though the rug had been ripped out from under me.

I have to give our line producer, Chris Olen Ray, major credit, as he was able to quickly find backup locations. They definitely weren't as cool as the navy base, but it was better than no locations. However, location changes meant I would have to scout, block, and film scenes on the same day. Certainly not ideal, but in the low-budget-movie world, these types of things happen. You have to roll with the punches.

What I hadn't expected was how big Mardi Gras was in Pensacola. Right as we were about to start shooting at the new locations, there was a massive Mardi Gras parade. At first, I was upset and concerned it would negatively affect our shoot. However, producers were smart enough to realize that it could add production value if we wrote some new scenes to take place at the parade. The decision was made, and the writers had new pages pouring in shortly.

I knew there would likely be a lot of people, but I didn't expect thousands of revelers with giant floats. The first shot we took was simple enough on paper: David Chokachi and Jackie Moore wave to the crowd from atop a float while in their army uniforms. It was nice character setup to show our heroes in a positive light.

So there I was, on a float surrounded by thousands of screaming people, two camera operators next to me, and focus pullers getting wireless video feeds tucked somewhere on the float. The sea of shouting voices was loud, and many in the crowd recognized David Chokachi. Some called out his real name, but the crowd was so loud the footage still worked. It didn't look like a fan shouting at a TV star, but a parade-goer celebrating a soldier. It looked big and expensive, so I was happy. This high-production-value sequence took some of the sting away from losing the actual navy base.

After the parade, the producers were told about a swanky governor's ball. Attendees would be dressed to the nines, and we were given permission to film there as long as all the guys wore tuxedoes, including me and the crew.

Making an expensive-looking movie requires expensive-looking things to happen in the frame. Every blockbuster movie has expensive sets and faces; they use expensive shots from expensive cameras and even more expensive lenses. If an opportunity arises to stage a scene somewhere that looks and feels expensive, do it. Take advantage.

The next thing I knew, I was getting fitted for a tuxedo. I hadn't worn one since I was a kid at some wedding. We rolled up with our dressy production crew and carried our gear into the opulent theater. The interior was decorated in Mardi Gras colors, and attendees enjoyed themselves behind fanciful masks. Right there, in the midst of this elegant party, we staged a scene between David Chokachi and Jackie Moore. It looked big and added production value, which was nice. Things were looking up, but it doesn't always shake out that way in the end.

After the high of the Mardi Gras party, we were filming a scene on a small street that we had shut down. The shot was simple: a government SUV fleeing a giant computer-generated sea creature. I needed the SUV to speed away as it was being chased, but a crew member raised a concern about one minor thing: a stop sign. Without a traffic cop to stop incoming cars, there was enough risk that we weren't permitted to go above the speed limit.

Every stunt, no matter how small, should appear on the permits you procure. Unfortunately I wasn't the one who filled out the permit, but I still had to shoot the script. It's my job to get the shot. If I don't get the shot in the script, I am not doing my job as a director.

Directing can be a hard job because you're forced to assert yourself, and that can be uncomfortable. It also means you're told no all the time, especially when directing low-budget movies. Can we put the camera on the sidewalk? No, that's not permitted. Can the actor drive the car? No, they are not allowed to drive and act. There are so many rules, and doing a movie that has action requires just as many permissions. You can't have an actor with a valid driver's license speed off in an SUV; you need a stunt coordinator, stunt driver, and traffic control. However, the town had given us permission to shut down the street, so I thought we were okay.

I never want anybody to get hurt on the set of a movie I'm making, but the risk seemed minimal. I was told the SUV had to stop at the sign; otherwise, we would be breaking the law. Story-wise, stopping made no sense. I had to get a shot of the SUV speeding away from the giant sea creature, so the vehicle had to blow past the damn stop sign.

Frustrated, I told the actor to stop at the stop sign, and he looked at me like I was a moron. "Why would I stop at a stop sign when I'm escaping for my life?" he asked. I agreed completely but our hands were tied because a crew member felt it was too dangerous for the SUV to run the stop sign.

After some internal moral debate, I told the actor to do what he felt his character would do. As far as I was concerned, it was a simple enough shot, and we had taken every precaution to make it as safe as possible. The actor slammed the gas, the SUV blazed through, and the shot looked great. Nobody got hurt, although the concerned crew member huffed and puffed and pointed at me, saying I was unsafe. I looked over to the *GQ* reporter taking notes and wondered if I would be portrayed as a reckless director in the article.

I thought that was the end of it, but when I got back to the hotel, the producers wanted to speak with me. I immediately regretted making that fucking SUV speed off. I got a tongue-lashing, and the producers were right. If something bad had happened, it would have been on them. They were not happy with my Dennis Hopper–inspired directing, and I agreed to play by the rules moving forward. The flame of my indie spirit was diminished.

The tension cleared after a few days, and other than standard behind-the-scenes drama, the shoot was a blast, the footage looked great, and the movie came together nicely in the edit. At the end of the day, that's what the audience cares about.

On location in Florida with actors Demetrius Stear and Graham Greene, for Atlantic Rim.

Prints and Advertising

❧

*A*tlantic *Rim* was released just days before the big-budget blockbuster *Pacific Rim*. Ironically, I was invited to an early screening of *Pacific Rim* that director Guillermo del Torro attended. I walked up to him and told him I directed a mockbuster called *Atlantic Rim*, to which he joked that I was taking his job. He's funny. *Pacific Rim* was amazing.

Pacific Rim got its massive studio marketing underway, with billboards and ads on buses and bus stops. *Atlantic Rim*, however, didn't have the same budget to work with, so I decided to get big "Atlantic" stickers made to cover the word *Pacific* on ads all over town. It was me against Hollywood, and with no real money to make it happen, I had to take matters into my own hands. To extend my reach, I snapped photos of my vandalism and posted the commandeered ads on my social media accounts.

I went to town, literally. A few people at a bus stop asked what I was doing as I slapped an "Atlantic" sticker on an ad. After I told them about the movie, they said they would check it out. My guerrilla marketing campaign was already working.

After targeting bus stops and movie theaters, I saw a moving bus in Santa Monica with a giant Pacific Rim ad splashed on the side by the beach. I was riding in the passenger seat, and my then-fiancé Sara, was driving. I told her to speed up and get as close to the bus as possible, which she did. At a red light, I jumped out of the car, sprinted to the bus, slapped an "Atlantic" sticker right on top of the word *Pacific*, and snapped a pic on my phone. Sara thought I was nuts, but I was having fun.

I repeated my sticker trick all over town and kept posting photos online, acting as if someone else was insane enough to do it. The response was not as validating as I'd hoped, but the posts got some traction, and that was enough. For me, it was a pure adrenaline rush, although I do not recommend the tactic. If a cop saw me, I'd probably have spent the night in jail. I imagine I pissed off at least one person who had to peel off those stickers.

Atlantic Rim came out, and I was pleasantly surprised when the response was bigger than expected. Maybe the sticker campaign actually worked! Shortly after, the *GQ* article came out, and you best believe that made for a great Facebook post. It felt nice to be featured in such a popular magazine.

The SyFy channel even chose to air *Atlantic Rim*, proof that it was gaining traction. In fact, the movie went on to become such a cult hit that *Mystery Science Theater 3000* did a full episode on it. It was surreal to see Patton Oswalt, Jonah Ray, Felica Day, and other big-name comedians talking about my movie on national television. Surely this meant I was coming up! Seeing your movie in the spotlight feels good, even if that moment is short-lived.

Although I was happy the movie was doing well, I wasn't immune to being knocked down a peg. One night when I was having a drink in Hollywood, I gushed to a stranger about *Atlantic Rim* and my marketing plan. All they said in return was, "Oh, so you direct B movies?" Ouch!

It was hard to accept that I was directing B movies. To me, they were much more. I truly tried my best to make the greatest version of whatever movie I was making. The fact that I was doing low-budget films and that some people would call them schlock wasn't a surprise, but they were still my projects, my work. I was grateful to have them in my life.

It was clear early on that I couldn't predict the kind of career I would have. I would have loved to be directing blockbuster movies with A-list celebrities, but I was still on the grind, and I wasn't about to stop.

Atlantic Rim, guerilla marketing.

Green Light, Red Light

After *Atlantic Rim* wrapped, I was back in LA writing scripts day and night. The more I wrote, the more I accomplished, and the better I felt. I was determined to start directing the next tier of movie, and I was finally gaining traction with the script I wrote after the *Traced* fiasco, *Reactor*.

I had managed to get *Reactor* in front of a legitimate company by sending off an email after a long night of IMDb trolling. A lot of connections have been made like this, with carefully crafted cold emails sent to the right person at the right company at the right time. After some back-and-forth, the company wrote up a rave coverage report and sent me an option agreement, which I happily signed. It was time to celebrate! *Reactor* would get made, and I was sure it would change my life instantly.

Just like before, that wasn't the case. Every few weeks, I'd receive an email saying the studio was waiting on a response from someone else before moving forward. My excitement waned. *Reactor* was dying a slow, painful death.

Time passed, and the option eventually expired without the movie getting made. It was a crushing blow, but it was softened when my phone rang with a new opportunity. A friend had passed my name along to a company looking to do a western full of horses and gunfights. This movie, *Stand Off*, seemed awesome, and the budget was bigger than anything I was used to. I signed the second the paperwork was in front of me. Although I'd never directed a western, *Tombstone* and *Young Guns* were two of my favorite movies, so I wasn't flying blind. Plus, the cast was set to be star studded, with Luke Perry as the lead. Luke and I even had a breakfast meeting at Jerry's, a famous deli.

I studied the *Stand Off* script, broke it down, and put in a lot of time preparing. Just as things looked to be shaping up and location scouting started, a quote came in from a local producer in Canada. It turns out Canada offers great rebates for filmmakers to incentivize shooting there. However, for the production to get the maximum rebate, the director, writer, and star all needed to be Canadian citizens. The more Canadians involved, the more money the company would get back. Well, the writer was Canadian, but I definitely wasn't, so I got booted off in exchange for someone with a Canadian passport. I would not be directing *Stand Off*; I would, in fact, be standing down—or rather sitting down in my apartment and pouring myself a drink.

That was the day I learned that signing a deal to make a movie does not mean you will actually be making that movie. Between *Reactor* going quiet and this western disappearing in a snap, I was feeling knocked down by a one-two punch.

I so badly wanted to do bigger projects, but the movie gods were keeping me firmly in place. There was only one thing I could do: update my demo reel. After cherry-picking the best shots from my movies, I managed to cut a slick reel for querying agents and managers. Querying is soul sucking by nature; you're practically begging them to look at your work and hoping they even bother to respond.

The few replies I did get were from reps telling me to stop directing low-budget movies. Hollywood is an aristocratic industry; the big studios are more likely to hire a first-time director with a win from a prestigious film festival than someone with a bunch of low-budget credits. It's all about words like *pedigree* or *prestige*. It is frustrating to be judged on the budget of the films you make, not the quality of what you did with that budget. As a low-budget filmmaker, I've found it's much harder to get respected by the big boys.

There is also an unfortunate stigma associated with budget levels in Hollywood. Some people say low-budget movies are not real movies. For the low-budget filmmaker, this is difficult to accept. I was told that low-budget movies were going to hurt my career in the long run, which is a hard pill to swallow when you want to make movies all the time. I decided to disregard their advice and continued to work and improve my craft. It was just old-guard mentality—aristocratic bullshit. I still think so, but I accept that this way of doing things isn't going to change.

I'd rather work than wait around for the phone to ring with some magical offer that may never come. Every movie I did was expanding my mental Rolodex of filmmaking knowledge. I was getting better, not worse. It's insane to think that someone with more experience would be looked down on, that an independent director would never be given a shot without an award. Between that and nepotism, Hollywood is deeply skewed to favor the wealthy.

I liked working. It was way better to be on a set making a movie than sitting on my ass, writing on spec, and smoking "hopium." If I kept grinding, I'd eventually carve my own path or die trying. I wasn't going to listen to some agent in Beverly Hills who wasn't representing me, telling me to turn down movies. I was going to work, not for the money, but because I enjoyed doing it and needed the outlet. Filmmaking kept me around interesting people. It had become my world, and I liked it. And if it was going to be my world, I would embrace it and give it all I had.

Bound (2015)

Whenever I was between movies, a slow wave of sadness would wash over me. I was now thirty and felt old. My family was supportive, but I wasn't where I imagined I would be ten years prior. When I was working, I was fine. For everyone who says happiness comes from within or whatever, that was not the case for me. I needed to be working to stay sane.

Because I read the trades, I knew that *Fifty Shades of Grey* was going into production soon. The book was already huge, and the movie would surely be marketed heavily. After doing a mockbuster of *Pacific Rim*, why not try doing a mockbuster for *Fifty Shades of Grey*? I wasted no time pitching my idea to the CEO of The Asylum, David Rimawi. To my delight, he didn't hate it, so I went to work on an outline without giving him time to change his mind.

At the time, I didn't know shit about the BDSM world because I'm not into getting whipped. However, the internet is an infinite resource of educational content. My browser history definitely got weird for a while, and for the next few months, I was served ads for ball gags and leather whips. I knew going into the movie that I would be entering uncharted territory, but that is the life of the filmmaker: to create different worlds and make them ring true.

After exploring the internet in my sex-themed crash course, I wrote a one-page treatment about a single mom who falls for a mysterious guy into BDSM. The guy turns out to be crazy, and her daughter gets caught up with him. It was a solid outline with a decent beginning, middle, and end. After going back and forth a few times with the development team, I got the nod to write the actual script.

As is typical when stepping outside my comfort zone, I struggled with the script for *Tied Down*. I didn't read the *Fifty Shades* book, and I didn't plan to. I didn't want to risk copying it subconsciously. I wanted to create something original. Just because it's a mockbuster doesn't mean the plot is at all similar—only the theme.

What I initially thought would be a challenge turned out to be almost impossible. This was an erotic thriller, and I had never written anything like that before. I started and stopped many times. I reworked and rewrote the hell out of it, but no matter what I did, it felt too edgy. It was just like writing *Bikini Spring Break*.

My first move was to rewatch movies I liked with a similar tone, like *Basic Instinct* and *Fatal Attraction*. This helped me get into the proper writing mindset so I could nail the tone. The plot was originally a murder mystery set in the BDSM scene, but once it got to the killings, it read more like horror than an erotic thriller. There was no point sending that version in, so I scrapped it. It needed to be sexier. I went the other way with the next draft, and it felt depraved. There was too much sex, but not in a sexy, sultry way—it just felt dirty. I was creatively off the mark, but nonetheless, I kept trying.

Every writer must face the moment when the deadline has come, and it's time to click "send." This was that moment of reckoning for me. You can't delay the inevitable, even if you don't love the draft.

The production team was kind when they said the script needed a more delicate feeling. I guess rape, drugs, and murder were a bit too extreme. I was getting nervous that they would shelve the project, but instead they brought in a fixer. Delondra Messa came to the rescue and lightened up the tone with her rewrite. She changed the title to *Bound*, and the script was finally approved for production.

Each genre has its own expectations, and a writer needs the right skill set to meet those expectations. Someone who is good at writing horror will probably not be able to write a great romantic comedy, but maybe they can. A lot of the original script, story, and characters were still in the movie, but it felt better, lighter, and more commercial.

During scouting, we looked at a real BDSM dungeon, and I gained a whole new appreciation for the community. There are rules and ethics involved, and those who choose that lifestyle abide by those rules. It's all respectful and taken very seriously.

This dungeon was hidden in plain sight under a seedy office building in the San Fernando Valley. It was a fully functional sex dungeon with every sex toy in sight, a giant leather cross, electric shocking devices, and a full-on human-sized cage. Being that I had zero experience in the BDSM world and was about to direct a movie about it, I took this opportunity to ask the leather-clad dominatrix about her work. She told me how she stomps on her clients' junk and spits on them, and they keep coming back for more. Her work was fascinating. In normal life, I would never be in a dungeon filled with sex toys, making that tour an experience I wouldn't soon forget.

After she talked about her work, I was a bit intimidated. I wanted *Bound* to be authentic to the BDSM world, but some of it was way too explicit and not what the producers were looking for. They wanted fun, sexy, and maybe a little dangerous; they did not want to see testicles tied up and getting electrocuted. I decided to follow the script as approved.

On the way out, the dominatrix suggested I set up an appointment with her for educational purposes. I'll admit that I thought about it, but since we were going for a light-hearted tone, there was no need for me to go full method actor. That said, we did book the location and hired the dominatrix as a consultant.

At that point, it was time to cast our two leads. The female lead wound up being an actress I grew up watching on *Buffy the Vampire Slayer*, Charisma Carpenter. I had a major crush on her when the show was on, so high school me was very proud. All those years later, she was still absolutely beautiful. It's always a trip meeting someone you grew up watching, but that excitement has to go away because you, as the director, have a job to do. No time to be a fanboy. Charisma has a strong, assertive presence that worked well for her businesswoman character. It also occurred to me that she was used to being on big-budget shows, so I did my best to make sure we were producing at the level she was accustomed to.

As exciting as this was, The Asylum wanted to put another star name in. As a filmmaker, you always want to work with stars, so when they told me they cast Daniel Baldwin, I was stoked. With more experience, I had become more confident as a director. I was engaging more with the cast and crew, asking more specific questions, and becoming an overall better movie director. At that point, I had also worked with most of the crew members and production staff before, so the set felt a bit more comfortable.

Things were going great until one of our lead actors got sick. It happens. Actors are human beings and sometimes they get sick, but on this day, that actor was in almost every scene. I didn't know what to do because I had a firm respect for the money being spent, so much so that I insisted on always shooting the maximum hours allotted for any given day. In my mind, if everyone was getting paid to work twelve hours, it would be ripping off the production to wrap early. All we got that day was one scene, and everyone went home. I felt uneasy.

If you wrap early, you're still going to get asked by producers if you're sure you got everything you needed for the day. It's a perfectly valid question, and you better be sure you got everything that day because if the editor finds a shot missing something in the review, it's not a good look.

You can always shoot more, but you can never go back in time. Well, you can do reshoots, but those are expensive, so it's best to get the shots you need and then some more to be sure.

On location for Bound.

Reflecting

I had built up a decent resume. People in the low-budget world knew me, there were some decent press articles out there, and I was still making new connections outside my network. I went to the American Film Market (AFM) every year, an annual event where the film industry descends on Santa Monica, California. For one week, hotel rooms turn into offices, and every major player in the game pulls the beds out of the room, brings in desks, and hangs up movie posters. It's pretty amazing. If you want to experience the heart of the movie business, AFM is it. Meetings take place all day, and lavish parties are hosted every night. Many times I found myself drunk off expensive free booze and going to party after party packed with industry people from across the world.

On the second-to-last day of AFM one year, I was hungover and running on fumes. I had been pitching my scripts all week to any company that would listen, so when my phone rang with an unfamiliar number, I wasn't sure who it could be. Besides, unless you're at the top of the film industry food chain, you pick up when someone calls, even if it's an unfamiliar number. It could be a producer or an agent or even an offer.

This time it was a guy named Richard Switzer, and he said he'd just seen *Born Bad* and wanted to make a movie with me. The finances were already in order, and he wanted me to direct. He had the voice of a forty-year-old and spoke with extreme confidence, but a call like this out of the blue felt too good to be true. With nothing to lose, I sent him a script titled *Buddy Hutchins*.

I wrote *Buddy Hutchins* years prior during one of my many writing binges. This script, full of nuance and intrigue, was about a guy who loses it one day and kills everyone around him. I loved the Michael Douglas movie *Falling Down* and hadn't seen anything like that since, so I wanted to write something in that vein. The story is simple: the world treats him like shit, and he gets revenge on everything. Although I was still skeptical of Richard, I was happy when he said he liked the script and was interested in making the movie.

Getting cold calls happens as a director, but usually it's some bullshitter who just wants to talk about making movies. But Richard confidently told me he would wire me fifty grand to get started. Nobody just wires someone fifty grand without meeting or video chatting. I thought for sure he was just another time waster, but I told him to send it.

The next day I woke up and found fifty thousand extra dollars in my account. My phone rang, and it was Richard excitedly asking me, "Did you get the money?"

With money to get started on *Buddy Hutchins*, I convinced my housemate John Mehrer to get on board to line produce. The line producer is one of the most important people in filmmaking because they control the lines of the budget. Every location booked, every actor hired—they all get paid by the line producer.

John was from Texas and was the type of guy who took no shit and got shit done. Without him behind the scenes, this movie wouldn't have come together as smoothly as it did. As John got to work, so did I, scouting locations and casting actors. We approached people we knew for this movie. No auditions—just offers to good actors who were right for the role.

Once you've done a few movies, you develop a roster of actors you like to work with. These are reliable, talented performers you can trust to show up and do a good job without giving you a headache. It's good to see what new talent is out there, but sometimes, when you really want to make sure there are no surprises, casting people you know works best. This is not to be confused with casting your friends. Your trusted roster should be real, talented actors who are right for the role and also happen to be friendly with you.

We wanted a star for the title role of *Buddy Hutchins*, someone who could sell the movie and pull off dark comedy, horror, and drama. Although I had pretty much stopped making videos at this point, I was still shooting for a few extra bucks between directing gigs. Every once in a while, I would be asked to shoot behind-the-scenes footage of other people's movies and do actor interviews on set. The BTS guy, as they call it. It was a fun gig that allowed me to meet and interview a lot of celebrities, one of which was Jamie Kennedy.

Jamie was cool when we met, so when we were looking for a star to play *Buddy Hutchins*, he came to mind. The production team agreed he was a solid choice, and Richard reached out with an offer. Not long after, I was summoned to Jamie's offices downtown. He wanted to meet me before saying yes or no. Just like before, Jamie was cool and even complimentary of the script. He was in. Everything was coming together great.

Take this as your sign that you need completed scripts in your back pocket. Opportunities come and go, and if I hadn't had a script ready when Richard called, he would've looked somewhere else. So, write, commission, or option scripts. Always have something solid ready to go because you never know who is going to come across your number. Besides, how can you call yourself a filmmaker if you don't have something ready to film?

We were lucky enough to cast Academy Award nominee Sally Kirkland as Jamie's mother. She, too, praised the script. It feels great when stars get excited about performing what you wrote. That energy promotes conversations about the characters, backstory, motivations, and things you never even thought about when writing the script. And you, the director, better be prepared to answer actors' questions when they come prepared with a script full of tabs, highlighted dialogue, and notes scribbled all over. Sally certainly did.

Richard Switzer and I still hadn't shaken hands before he arrived in LA for the shoot. From our phone conversations, I was convinced he was some middle-aged doctor or lawyer, but in walks this skinny eighteen-year-old kid with a forty-year-old's voice. *Child prodigy* is the term I would use for him because he managed to put together *Buddy Hutchins* and another movie at eighteen years old. Shortly after, he became a highly successful producer while being younger than anyone I knew in that role.

By the end of a shoot, directing often feels like a blur, and this was no different with *Buddy Hutchins*. I find myself surprised when I watch candid videos of me directing. The energy I exert is high level and nonstop. Excess weight falls off during every movie I direct because I'm spending so much time moving and talking. I'm rapid-fire answering questions and shouting directions to everyone around me, constantly adjusting or pushing the pace of the set. I need everything to be exactly how I want it and often shoot without so much as a second of pause. After my time as a whirling dervish, I sit down in my director's chair and stare intently at the monitor, call cut, and then do it all again. Directing is tiring, but you don't feel it until the end. Then you're exhausted.

Like all the movies I did, I thought *Buddy Hutchins* was going to be *it*. Exactly like those other times, I still wasn't right.

The editing process went efficiently considering the editor, Jessica, was living in our garage at the time. I spent a month in there, smoking weed and going through each scene over and over until it felt right. I really did feel good about this movie. It had a uniqueness that I thought gave it a chance to break out. Unfortunately, the audience didn't get it. Without an expensive marketing campaign or a big release, it quickly evaporated into the ether. You can still find it, but you'll surely have to type it in the search bar. In my opinion, it's criminally underrated, but maybe one day it will find an audience.

In between scenes with the star of Buddy Hutchins, Jamie Kennedy.

God's Club (2015)

M y last name, Cohn, is quintessentially Jewish, so I was a little surprised when my name came up to direct a Christian movie. I'm not Orthodox or strictly religious, but I am spiritual, so I had no reservations about the subject matter. I believe in karma and that things happen for a reason, and this opportunity landed before me, so it must have been meant to be. Besides, I'm all for positive messages and, of course, making movies.

The script was dialogue heavy compared to the suspense, action, and horror movies I had worked on prior. There were no crazy stunts, but I had the same number of days to film, which gave me more time to make the shots count. As a bonus, I would be working with star name again, which always made a shoot feel more real to me. On *Bound* we had Daniel Baldwin, for *God's Club* I would have the pleasure of working with his brother, Stephen Baldwin.

Lorenzo Lamas from Renegade was also cast, which was cool because I grew up watching him. We also snagged Corbin Bernsen who played in *The Dentist*, one of my favorite horror movies.

Stephen Baldwin, a very faithful guy already, was really into the movie's message. He is a passionate actor who gives every performance his all and dives deep into his character, which I respect. Many of Stephen's lines contained lengthy biblical passages that he was adamant about getting exactly right. It's a reasonable concern for an actor to have because if something is off, it's the actor's face on screen, and they'll take the heat.

The only problem was we were shooting a pivotal scene of him speaking to his daughter—and the sun was going down. The scene was supposed to take place during the day. We had to get the shot, or we would lose our light and not make the schedule. Not making your day as the director is the worst. The producers often have to pay to bring everyone back to make up the scene, and they might do it with another director.

As time passed, I grew nervous because I wasn't sure we would have enough light. But what could I do? I wasn't about to demand Stephen come out and perform a complex, two-page monologue before he was ready. Each actor has their process, and to hinder them would be hindering the movie.

Despite having a script supervisor, it was up to Stephen to make sure the words he said lined up with the Bible. If he misquoted it, he would get the egg on his face, not me. Had I anticipated this challenge, I would've made sure to meet up to go over the script. We could've gone line by line to make sure everything was dialed in before we got to set. Even though I did not write the script, it's the director's job to make sure everything runs smoothly so the movie gets completed.

With more time I might have gotten a few more angles on some scenes, but we got exactly what we needed, and *God's Club* turned out to be a solid movie.

At this point, my process of working with the editor had also tightened up. It also helped that I was working with editors who knew my style and the way I shot, so everything moved a little bit smoother.

On location with the stars of God's Club, Lorenzo Lamas, Stephen Baldwin and Corbin Bernsen.

Still Rolling!

⁓

The funny thing about making movies is that as soon as you wrap, not only do you have a movie in the can, but you are also officially unemployed again.

I always put extreme pressure on myself to keep moving between movies. Every morning I woke up and asked myself, "What can I do to be productive today?" In reality, this kept me in a constant state of disappointment because whatever I was doing wasn't good enough. If I wrote a script, I couldn't be happy until I sold it, and then I wouldn't be happy until I was making it, and even then, I wouldn't be happy until it got good reviews. It never ended.

With postproduction finished, *God's Club* came out and was approved by the Dove Foundation, whatever that is worth. It certainly made for a good Facebook post. But now that *God's Club* was behind me, it was time to get my next job.

I had fully accepted that I was now a director and that my days of acting were over. But then I got a call asking if I wanted to audition to play the role of "director" in a mockumentary of the making of *Sharknado*, called *Sharknado: Heart of Sharkness*. At this point, *Sharknado* was a global phenomenon, so of course I wanted in. Plus it was an opportunity to act, and part of me still missed it. It was my shot at redemption, so it was easy to accept the audition.

Determined to win the role, I stayed up all night, running lines with my then-fiancé Sara. The next day I was in The Asylum casting room, which felt a bit less familiar now that I was back on the other side of the table. I gave it my best go and went right back to my days of being an anxious actor, waiting to hear if I landed a part or not. I realized this part of acting, the anxiety, was something I did not miss. It was hard to turn off my brain and stop thinking about it. You work so hard and become the character for a few minutes in the audition, and that affects your whole being for days. I told myself that whether or not I got the role, I would be okay. I was a real director; I didn't need to play one. But I still wanted the role.

When you're waiting for an answer, your brain can come up with all kinds of rationalizations, like "It's not meant to be." But the truth is every actor who auditions wants the part. Every director who takes the meeting wants the movie. We all want the job. Luckily, this time I got it. Alongside me were Rachel True (Mary Jane from *Half Baked*), Julie McCullough, Zack Ward, Scotty Mullen, and fellow director James Cullen Bressack. It was a crew of filmmakers and actors, acting as a crew of filmmakers and actors.

I embodied the role of the obsessed filmmaker, playing an exaggerated version of myself. I was running around town, barking eccentric direction for my art-house version of *Sharknado*. I threw laptops, I was running into the ocean—basically doing silly shit that I normally don't get to do.

We were making a movie within a movie, and the result, *Sharknado: Heart of Sharkness*, turned out really funny. As a bonus, I can now say I starred in an official *Sharknado* movie. It was great to just act for once instead of having to direct.

It was a fun experience, but *Heart of Sharkness* didn't blow up like the other *Sharknado* movies. Perhaps fellow filmmakers would appreciate a behind-the-scenes movie more than a regular audience.

Either way, it was back on the grind.

Acting in Sharknado: Heart of Sharkness.

Making Moves

At some point in every director's career, they want to produce because they know the producer is the one really in charge. I had produced *And So They Die*, *Underground Lizard People*, and *Hulk Blood Tapes* years back, and while those movies were not financial successes, I still believed I could make a movie and turn a profit. But wanting it didn't mean I could snap my fingers and make myself a producer. First, I hit the books to do what I always do: study.

Gabriel Campisi wrote a great book on putting together business plans for independent filmmakers. I didn't know him when I read his book, but I shot him a message on Facebook afterward. In it, I praised his book and discussed making a movie together. Luckily, he was game.

I spoke with my longtime actor and producer friend Demetrius Stear and set up a meeting between the three of us, where we decided to produce a movie together. We would pool our resources and collectively finance and produce it. There was just one thing we needed: a script.

Well, I had hard drives filled with scripts. The one I ended up pitching was conceived when my housemate John Mehrer and I were wasted and spitballing movie plots for fun. It was a story about a serial killer named Johnny who drowns people in their own pools, aptly called *The Valley Drowner*. Johnny goes on to become a social media star due to his good looks, sort of like a modern Ted Bundy. It was a quirky, original concept, and I was pleased that both

Demetrius and Gabriel liked the script. We cut a deal among ourselves and set out to make *The Valley Drowner.*

We needed a lot of locations, but finding locations in LA sucks. Outside of LA, people will practically offer their homes to movie crews for free. LA folks, on the other hand, are savvy and know a location's worth and that a C-stand will probably ding their wall.

We wanted to spend next to nothing and shoot the movie in nine days, which is sort of mission impossible. However, with careful corner-cutting and a guerrilla-filmmaking mentality, we marched on unrelenting. We teamed up with the king of microbudget movies, David Sterling, who helped us find amazing locations on the cheap.

Rather than spending fifteen dollars a head for lunch, Sterling ordered pizzas and Subway sandwiches. Instead of working with a crew of thirty or forty, we had ten. We risked it and skipped out on permits, which saved a lot of money. This was a nonunion movie, meaning it was not SAG, so we would also not have to pay for a payroll company. There's a reason David Sterling is the master of the low-budget movie. He really knows how to stretch a dollar.

The one drawback of guerrilla filmmaking is that even when you're hidden inside a house, a police officer can knock on the door and shut you down at any moment. Maybe you took up all the parking on the street, so the neighbor complained and called the cops. That anxiety, while thrilling, also takes a toll. You may save money, but you're signing that bill one way or the other.

Another thing about making a movie on an insanely tight schedule is you miss the extra days. With only nine days to make a feature-length movie, we had no choice but to move super-fast. The amount of time we had to shoot a scene was limited, so our coverage was limited. Our setups were reduced to run on a tighter timeline. Nothing could go wrong.

It takes more experience to pull off a stunt like this, and I doubt I would have been able to at the beginning of my career. I could move so fast because I knew exactly what shots I needed and how long it would take. I was constantly recalculating our time to take advantage of every moment we had. A good director is someone who makes days. They know how much time they have per scene, how long the wardrobe changes take, how long art or hair needs, and so on. Ultimately the goal is to make a great movie, so if you can make days and make a great movie, then you might have a chance at succeeding in the long run.

As much as I love having a full crew and sitting back in my director's chair at video village, there is something special about guerrilla filmmaking. Breaking the rules always comes with an exciting rush. Don't get me wrong, I'll take a proper crew and permits over a skeleton crew and carrying gear myself any day. I don't like worrying about getting shut down. But doing *The Valley Drowner* like this brought me back to my film school days and stealing shots for music videos.

At the end of the movie, Randy Wayne's Johnny runs away from the cops and jumps into the Los Angeles River to escape. It was a great ending, but finding someone willing to jump into that polluted mess was going to be tough. The water was a murky brownish green, filled with trash and who knows what else. The whole thing reeked of rotten eggs. After scouting around, we found an access point under an overpass that seemed cinematic. It was perfect for the scene, but the water was gnarly. Luckily, we knew a fearless stuntman who agreed without batting an eye.

The stunt double wore a copy of our hero's wardrobe and jumped right into the disgusting LA River while holding his breath, no hesitation. The final shot came out perfectly. When he came back up drenched in muck and smelling like shit, we gave him a huge round of applause and poured fresh water on him. What a champion.

At wrap, I almost couldn't believe we had pulled it off. We had come together and made a movie on our own, without getting shut down or anyone getting hurt. That's a win any day. We were really happy with ourselves for staying on budget and shooting the movie in nine days. We were so confident that we would at the very least recoup what we spent that we thought, "What better time to double down and make another movie following the same model, but this time for even less?"

*Sara Malakul Lane, Randy Wayne and DP Josh Maas on The Valley
Drowner*

The Domicile (2017)

〜

Since we had just spent a lot of money on expensive locations for *The Valley Drowner*, we decided to do a horror movie set in one location to save money. We found a big house in Old Pasadena. It was perfect—huge, with high ceilings and an old wooden staircase, and packed with Victorian furniture. It was the exact kind of creepy house you want in a one-location ghost movie.

After locking in the house, it was time to write a script that suited the location. It quickly became clear that writing a script for one location was much more challenging than expected. I was up against the same challenge as when I wrote *Legend Has It* many years before. Writing a good script with a bunch of locations is hard enough and without locations to expand the story, I threw in every horror trope and jump scare I could.

Out came the script for *The Domicile*, a very formulaic ghost story. Not bad, just completely unoriginal.

We assembled the same crew from *The Valley Drowner* and started shooting. We started filming, and the old house looked beautiful, the ghost makeup was solid, and the acting and cinematography were on point. Despite relying on every trope in the book, *The Domicile* was shaping up to be a solid low-budget horror movie.

In one of the many jump scares, our lead actor needed to get spooked by the ghost and fall backward down the steep, hardwood staircase. Prior to the shoot, we had prepared for this scene and hired a professional stunt performer to do the fall. Well, on the day we planned to film the stair fall, our stunt performer's car broke down, and he was unable to get to the set. We still needed to get the shot, so I volunteered to do the stunt myself out of necessity.

A proper stuntman would have worn a back brace and pads on their elbows and knees. They'd have had a thick crash pad to land on. I didn't have any of that. The character was wearing only a bathrobe, so I wore only a bathrobe and managed to find an air mattress to land on at the bottom of the stairwell.

The crew thought I was nuts for trying, but we needed the shot, and I was the only person on set about the same height and size as our lead actor, Steve Richard Harris. I knew if the fall was fast enough, you wouldn't be able to tell it was me. I had two cameras lined up as I mustered up the courage to throw myself down the steps. In my mind, I rationalized that we needed this to sell the movie. Suddenly it became an important personal challenge.

I called out for the cameras to roll as I stood atop the stairs and looked down at my concerned fiancé, Sara. I don't remember calling action, but I took a breath and hurled myself down the stairs. *Bump, bang, boom!* My elbow smashed into a step, and I crashed onto the air mattress, bursting it. I stood up, rocked but not hurt, and proud of myself. I checked the playback on the cameras, and although it looked cool, you could still sort of tell it was me. In order to sell this gag better, we would need another angle, and that meant another shot. We adjusted the camera positions for a second take, and once again the crew thought I was out of my mind.

Adrenaline pumped through my veins as I walked back to the top of the stairwell. I looked down, said a little prayer, and launched myself back down. I told myself, "The scarier the stunt, the better the movie, and the more it would sell for." This was a trailer moment, I knew it. As I tumbled this time, I managed to smash my other elbow and twist my ankle.

Lying at the bottom of the steps, flat on my back and disoriented, I was still proud. A challenge had arisen, and I went for it. There was some pain, but that was okay. Nothing broke, everything worked. That was the last time I did a stunt like that, and I wouldn't recommend anyone following my footsteps. That was just how I rolled—literally.

That night I went home and iced my entire body, which was turning stunning shades of purple and blue. Little did I know the pain was just beginning.

Preparing to throw myself down the stairs on The Domicile

Distribution 101

With our two movies edited, we had two opportunities to cash in through distribution. At least that's what I thought.

Between *The Valley Drowner* and *The Domicile*, Gabriel, Demetrius, and I had spent quite a bit of money. Despite the drain on my bank account, I was confident we would find a distributor and make it back. Both movies were solid and looked high quality, so I sent them out to some people I met at AFM, the American Film Market. Not a single person bit.

The movies were rejected by the top companies, and no one offered a cent up front for either. It was heartbreaking. I had been convinced some distributor would offer us something, but nope. The reality was the movies didn't have big stars, and without stars, it's difficult to get a minimum guarantee or any money up front.

We moved on to the companies that would do a distribution split, meaning they would take a percentage of the sales but give no advance. Once we zeroed in on a company that had distributed some pretty good titles, I went to their offices to see if I could negotiate a deal for our two titles. I busted out one of my nicer button-down shirts and made sure I looked presentable. I wanted to be taken seriously; it was crucial that we at least recoup our costs if we wanted to stay in business.

After a warm greeting, I was shown a sales projection estimating how much the movie would earn in each territory, such as Spain or Canada. According to their projections, we were looking to make hundreds of thousands of dollars, maybe more if they sold both movies to a number of territories. I got excited. They suggested we change the title of *The Valley Drowner* to *Death Pool* to ride the *Deadpool* wave, and reluctantly, I agreed. I figured they knew best, and I wanted the numbers on the sales projection sheet to come true.

Looking back, I wish we would've pushed back on the title change. I absolutely hate the name *Death Pool*. It will always be *The Valley Drowner* to me.

While both movies got picked up by Redbox and Tubi, were available on VOD, and sold as DVD and Blu-ray, we weren't seeing a dime. I knew for a fact both movies were making money and was expecting the checks to show up in the mail. I thought we had figured out a way to make money while making our own movies. With that sustainable business model, we would be shooting again shortly. I was dead wrong. It was a financial disaster.

For years, we didn't see a penny. Instead we would occasionally receive financial statements that were improperly formatted and not on time. It was heartbreaking to be treated so awfully. It later came out that our sales agent cut a deal with a distributor that gave them the majority of the money. Apparently, we allowed them to do this and draft whatever kind of deal they wanted—it was all in the fine print. We should've never allowed it to happen, but we were desperate. When all the other options had evaporated, it seemed like the only move we could make. In hindsight, we would've been better off self-distributing or selling copies out of the back of my car.

I hated having to send aggressive emails just to figure out what the hell was going on. Eventually we saw a small sum of money followed by a few more minuscule payouts. We never came close to regaining the cost of one movie. It was a total loss.

It's disappointing to see your movies all over and not get a penny, but we took a risk and lost big. If you're going to make a movie without a buyer attached, you're making that movie on spec, which is a big risk. You can for sure get a minimum guarantee if you have a big star, but you need money to get the star plus the money to make the movie. You either need the star or the money to get things going, and at a certain point, you need both.

The Hollywood system is a catch-twenty-two, so people usually wind up making a movie with no stars for barely any money and hope it will sell. Sometimes it works out, but sometimes it doesn't, and you lose. Unfortunately more often than not, the filmmaker loses. Beware of sales agents or distributors who make big promises; there are a lot more people who've lost than won. There's an entire Facebook group called Movie Distributors to Stay Away From and Why. It's filled with horror stories from filmmakers.

These failures hurt way worse than those stairs I threw myself down. It sucks to lose money, and I felt bad for getting Demetrius and Gabriel into that kind of scenario. I felt defeated. I still couldn't crack the producing code. Maybe it just wasn't meant to be. Either way, I had spent all my money, so I was back to the grindstone. I had bills to pay.

Little Dead Rotting Hood (2015)

$\approx\sim$

Losing all your money feels like shit. Thankfully, Gabriel Campisi had written a cool werewolf script called *Little Dead Rotting Hood*, a horror take on "Little Red Riding Hood." The script was wild, full of werewolves and evil spirits. He had taken the project to The Asylum, and it was right up their alley, and I was grateful to Gabriel and The Asylum for the chance to direct it.

I was pumped to be working again and to have something to do during the day. When you're working on a movie, it consumes you. You don't have the free time to let your mind wander to how dumb you were for blowing all your money on two movies that didn't make a cent.

That said, Gabriel's script had its challenges. It read as if it were a $100 million movie, but we had far less than that to work with.

As director, you take on the responsibility of delivering what's on the page, whether you have the resources, the know-how, or not. You have to film something, and that something has to be good.

My experience with giant sea creatures and robots on *Atlantic Rim* helped tremendously on this project. The script had all sorts of tricky shots I'd have to work out with VFX-like characters transforming into wolves and killing other people. After discussing the sheer amount of visual effects needed, I decided to shoot with real wolves, so the VFX department didn't have to spend time generating them. Doing this meant they could spend more time creating the giant wolf at the end, which had to be computer generated.

However, having real wolves on set isn't a cheap option either. In addition to the wolf, you need a handling team to keep people safe. Luckily The Asylum was on board and agreed real wolves were the way to go. I had some talks with the wolf handler and learned as much as I could about what the wolves were permitted to do. It turned out the wolves could move from point A to point B and snarl, but they could not simulate an attack, not even on their handler, because they were too wild. This created a new problem: the script was filled with people getting mauled by wolves. If all those shots had to be VFX, that would be the VFX budget for the whole film, and that would not work.

I thought about using big, wolf-like dogs for the actual attack shots. I thought if it was dark enough, we could use quick edits to make it work. It turned out the animal handlers had Belgian Malinois dogs we could use. They were big and could jump on people, bite down on a bite sleeve, and do all sorts of other cool tricks that the wolves couldn't. A new plan came together to combine the wolves with the dogs. Dogs came from wolves after all, so it was full circle! The idea was to film the wolves approaching and have them run past the camera so the next shot could be a dog jumping on a guy and taking him down. Once on the ground, I would get a close-up of the dog's mouth pulling on the guy. We even got an authentic wolf-head puppet to sneak in there for some additional close-ups.

I was feeling good until I was sent photos of the available dogs and wolves. Some of the dogs had tan fur, but the wolves were all black. How were we going to use a tan dog to double as a black wolf? That wouldn't look right.

My next call was to the hair department to ask if there was a safe way to dye the dog's coats. We found a temporary spray-on, nontoxic hair color, and it worked perfectly. Now we had a full game plan for the action sequences. I just hoped nobody would get hurt.

We lined up a star-studded cast with Romeo Miller (Lil' Romeo), Eric Balfour, Patrick Muldoon, Marina Sirtis, Bianca Santos, Heather Tom, and Brendan Wayne. I am a huge *Star Trek* fan so when we landed Marina Sirtis, who played Counselor Troi, I geeked out a bit. I proudly showed her the Klingon trefoil tattoo on my arm. Not sure she was impressed.

At the time, this movie was big budget for me. There was even an extra trailer on set that was all mine—someone put my name on it. While that part was cool, I was way too busy to have any downtime to enjoy it. Perhaps on bigger movies, directors have the leisure to kick back, but my time in the trailer was limited to poking my head in and snapping a selfie before going back to work.

While shooting, one of our actors kept using a subtle accent, which I thought worked great and added to the small-town feel of his character. However, after viewing the dailies, one of the producers was not a fan. I suddenly found myself in the predicament of having to tell an actor to cut out part of their characterization. You never know if an actor has spent a lot of time creating their persona and developing their voice. I tried to talk to him about dropping the accent, but he continued to use it in every take. After a few more attempts to get him to stop, I gave up because he was clearly committed to the accent regardless of what I said or did. I lost that battle and took some heat from the producers for not being able to make it happen.

When the wolves showed up, it was amazing to see how massive they and their teeth were. The handlers set up a perimeter and roped off an area where wolves would be allowed, and nobody was to touch the wolves or get anywhere near them.

And then the giant dogs showed up, painted black and looking like the beasts we needed. We had some safety meetings about keeping away from the animals, and then it was time to shoot. The wolves went first and performed amazingly before it was time for the dogs to jump on people and attack. We carefully positioned the camera and moved the lights to darken the image further to create the illusion of actual wolves. They tackled the actors, and it came out super awesome. I knew the shots would match nicely in the edit. I was feeling good, and nobody got hurt—until they did.

I was rehearsing with the actors for the next shot, when a production coordinator rushed toward us to say one of the stunt performers was attacked by a wolf. Apparently, he had approached the wolf handler, claiming to have worked with wolves before and wanting to interact. Despite being told not to touch the wolves, the stunt performer reached out, and the wolf bit down and wouldn't let go. The exact phrasing was that it "mauled the shit out of his arm." The stuntman was taken away in an ambulance with his bicep dangling off. I hoped the guy would be okay. I felt bad, but I had no choice but to keep filming. There's only so much you can do when someone refuses to listen. The show must go on.

Luckily, nobody else was hurt. Afterward, the VFX team went to work transforming people into wolves and creating a megawolf for the final showdown. I thought it was a fun movie, and we even had a premiere, complete with a performer in a werewolf suit. For that one evening, the movie was the talk of the town. However, there's always somebody else's movie coming the next night.

As a director, you think you're advancing in your career by accumulating movie titles, but that is not the case until you have a hit. Only then can things advance. For the low-budget movie director without representation or famous parents, the only way forward is to keep grinding and keep on keeping on.

Hanging with one of our picture animals and handler on location of Little Dead Rotting Hood.

Devil's Domain (2016)

Although I was working nonstop, I still didn't feel like I'd made it. But I also began to realize I'd never liked that expression. To this day, I think I function better when I feel like I'm in the trenches. I don't want to get too comfortable. Part of me likes the grind, the hunger. It's fuel.

I had done a faith-based movie and movies about a serial killer, an evil baby, a werewolf, and girls in bikinis. Naturally, it was time to make a movie about the devil.

One of my good friends, Brian Perera, is the CEO of Cleopatra Records. Cleopatra Records is a successful independent record label that was founded in 1996 and has been associated with amazing artists like Jane's Addiction, DMX, and 311. Brian, who looked like a young Mick Jagger and who *LA Weekly* called the Goth Lord, had made some horror movies in the past and wanted to make another one. This time, he had a demonic idea for the story.

As we sat in his goth-themed, rock-and-roll office, sipping some Jack Daniels, we came up with a movie about a girl who sells her soul to the devil. However, our devil was a beautiful seductress who would seduce this girl and get her revenge on the mean girls cyberbullying her at school. With this idea, I was sent off to pen the script.

I rolled some spliffs, poured a glass of whiskey, and planted my ass in front of my laptop for what turned out to be weeks of binge-writing sessions. Once I started, I had to finish.

I had people waiting for me to turn in my first draft of *Devil's Domain*. Screenwriting feels different when you have someone waiting to read your script, especially when that someone runs a successful company and wants to finance the movie. When writing on spec, though, you have every reason in the world to procrastinate. There's no deadline, and it leads you to question if you really are a professional writer.

The harsh truth is, if you don't have contacts and nobody is paying you, you're essentially a hobbyist writer. To this day it's still hard for me to write on spec. Finding the motivation to create something new when I have fifty or so unproduced scripts sitting on hard drives is tough. Why should I? I can just dig up an old script, rewrite it, and try and get that one made. It's always a mental battle to start something new.

That's not how a real writer behaves though. I struggled to call myself a writer even after twenty-one of my scripts were made into movies. How we see ourselves isn't usually how others do. I was afraid of failure, and my measurement for success was constantly changing. The goalpost continued to move down an endless field. Would I ever call myself a successful filmmaker? I preferred working and not thinking about it. In my mind, only a Michael Bay level of success was real because he got to blow up expensive shit. I wanted to do that too.

I stared at the ninety-five pages of *Devil's Domain* after attaching it to an email to the producers. The script was solid, but it's always nerve-racking sending one off. It wasn't as bad as the first time I sent a draft for feedback, but the anxiety still reared its ugly head. It seems like the more things change, the more they stay the same. It's like no matter how much you work, you still think this movie could be your last, and you start to worry. There is always a chance they'll read the script and scrap the project—it happens all the time. Writers are hired, fired, and replaced. Everyone is replaceable. Even actors get cut out sometimes. It's a fear that never goes away.

You can either worry yourself to death on every movie you do, or you can just click send on the draft. If they hate it, they hate it.

Much to my delight, Brian did not hate this one, but he did want a higher body count, which I addressed by killing off almost every character in the movie. With my extra-violent script approved, we held auditions and found some talented actors. Still, we needed the devil girl. Some good actresses had given us their best devil rendition, but nobody quite nailed it.

Suddenly a tall, stunning French model poked her head into the casting studio. We asked her if she was ready, and she asked to have a cigarette first, which I thought was very European. Linda Bella looked like she'd stepped right out of a magazine and into the real world. Her French accent was sexy, not too thick, and she nailed the audition to become our devil.

When an actor comes in and crushes it, it's reinvigorating. You know that's the person you want, and you get a glimpse at what the film could be. The audition is also sometimes the first time you hear your words spoken by an actor instead of inside your brain. Sometimes you are pleasantly surprised, and sometimes you realize another dialogue pass might be in order.

Despite having talented actors who were right for their roles, the producers wanted star power to help sell the movie. This was music to my ears. They wanted the right person to play the tough dad character, and the producers were willing to pay.

One of my favorite actors of all time is Michael Madsen; I find his raspy voice and soft-spoken yet intimidating presence compelling. Michael was the star of the masterpiece *Reservoir Dogs* and other Quentin Tarantino movies. I'll admit I am a fan of Tarantino, as he is possibly the most knowledgeable filmmaker of all time. Listening to Tarantino speak about films and filmmaking is like listening to Bob Ross talking about painting. Tarantino sees everything, understands the importance of shots and characters, and can ensure it all plays together. He is a master of his craft and truly understands the importance of style. It is because of him I watch old movies even when I can't stand the slower pacing or bizarre transatlantic accent. I watch and absorb what I can.

As much as I wanted Michael Madsen, getting to an actor you want is always a challenge, even with the right money. You can find contact info on IMDbPro, but that's usually a general number for an assistant who maybe, hopefully, can get you to someone who can actually help. If these people have no idea who you are, they will take their time getting back.

After some back-and-forth, we finally spoke to the right person to get the script and offer on Madsen's desk.

When an actor says they are going to read a script, there's no other choice but to wait. They may never get back to you, or you may have to nudge them several times, but there is nothing you can do to speed up this process. It's tempting to charge forward, line everything up and hope it all works out, but that's costly if it falls through. Producers and casting directors put expiration dates on offers, but that's usually just for show. As hard as it may be, you just have to be patient unless you have a lot of money. Then the rules change, as they always do. Especially in this town.

It was exciting to hear that Madsen read the script and liked the role. After some negotiation, he was in. Hearing his iconic voice over the phone was a nostalgic reward of its own. We talked shop about his character and the kind of wardrobe he'd wear. Wardrobe can be an important discussion topic because what you have in mind for the look doesn't always match what the actor will like. Star actors are often particular about the type and cut of the clothes they wear. The last place you want to be is on set with an actor refusing to wear anything in wardrobe. You may think they look great, but if they hate it, you're going to be stuck waiting while someone else frantically shops for replacements. When possible, it's always good to do everything wardrobe related well before you shoot. Otherwise, show up with a lot of options in different sizes.

The production was required to provide lodging for Madsen, which is standard when dealing with stars. I was asked to provide suggestions for nearby hotels since I was familiar with the area. A quick online search gave me a couple of results, and I presented them to the team. Of course, they were all high-end, expensive accommodations befitting a star of his caliber.

The night before Madsen's first day, I got a phone call informing me that he wouldn't be staying at the hotel we booked. According to Madsen's camp, the place looked like a "detention center." Production had not listened to any of my suggestions for nice, expensive hotels. Instead they cheaped out and now had to pay the price and scramble to find something suitable. I looked at photos of the hotel they tried to get this world-renowned movie star to stay in, and he was right: it did look like a detention center!

I introduced myself when he showed up to the set but was far too busy to geek out. We chatted for a minute, and then he was off to "go through the works," meaning get wardrobed up and through hair and makeup.

It's rewarding when you find yourself directing and look at the monitor to see one of your favorite actors. The same Michael Madsen that starred in Tarantino movies was starring in my movie. I wanted to pinch myself, but there was already so much going on that it was hard to fully appreciate the situation. That would wait until I was lying in bed that night, realizing I just directed Mr. Blonde.

The AD I worked with for this film had a weird way of doing things. The AD is responsible for keeping the director on schedule, but this guy had a clever way of manipulating me into wrapping early by constantly telling me we were behind schedule. On day one, he told the DP and me that we were hours behind schedule, so I did what I normally would and sped up to make time. Working hastily is never the right move because rushing makes the work suffer. I made the mistake of trusting him, and after rushing scenes before lunch, I discovered we had shot everything for that day. I was pissed. I had sped through scenes that would never be reshot. After that, I moved at my own pace and made sure I never worked with that AD again.

The relationship between the AD and director can absolutely make or break your experience on set. The assistant director "runs the set," as is often said, meaning all departments communicate with the director through the AD. This valuable information, however, can be filtered, altered, or sometimes not passed on at all.

The AD's attitude can also dictate the tone of the set. Moods can be raised or lowered by choices the AD makes, and the tone they set can affect actor morale, which is extremely sensitive. Actors are putting themselves out there and want to know the production cares about making a good movie. Dealing with actors is an art in itself; it takes years of experience to understand the idiosyncrasies that might impact a shoot. If a movie ends up sucking, an actor's career might take a hit, while an AD can go right on to the next show.

Cast grumpiness is also different from crew grumpiness. Being part of a cast is a weird job. It can be uncomfortable if you don't gel with the people around you. However, I'll never understand a crew member who constantly complains, especially in the low-budget world where people can make more money working fewer hours somewhere else. You have to enjoy this kind of work. If you don't, don't do it. It's certainly not going to get any easier.

One night on set, we were filming on the front lawn of a house in Northridge around midnight. Out of nowhere, three police cars rolled up, lights twirling and spotlights blazing. Annoyed at being stopped, I called out that we had permits and stormed toward the blinding red and blue lights. The cops yelled back at me, but I couldn't make out their words, so I kept walking toward them. The next thing I saw were several guns pointed right at me. It was then I finally heard a clear voice.

"Get down on your fucking knees! Face down, arms out!"

I looked around, and everyone else behind me was already complying. Dazed by the light smashing into my face and the loud overlapping voices, it took me a moment to do the same. I was lucky to not be shot. It turned out a neighbor thought there was a break-in and called the cops.

By the time we finished the shoot, nobody was shot, at least not by a gun. Afterward, as sometimes happened at the end of a movie, I got sad. I'm not sure if it's the adrenaline dump or what, but more often than not, I don't know what to do with myself for a few days after finishing a movie. You use so much energy on set, and returning to normal life is a shock to the system. Accepting that a movie is over and that you're once again unemployed is also part of it.

Of course, I worked on the cut with the editor, but I find editing nowhere near as engaging as directing. When *Devil's Domain* was finished, we held a screening, and at the end, we got a thundering applause. The movie truly turned out awesome but, unsurprisingly, did not get anywhere near the amount of hype it deserved.

Having movie after movie get released only to seemingly evaporate is disheartening. So much work went into those movies, and they would just be available online somewhere. If I was lucky, they would maybe get a press article or two. Sometimes, though, there was nothing.

I suspect thirty years ago it was more of an event when a movie came out. However, dozens of independent movies are released every day now. It is no longer a big, special thing. People don't care as much because there are so many options. I almost felt like I was painting a picture and then just putting it in a drawer and never looking at it again.

Months passed without a new movie project. I tried writing, but my motivation was gone. I had dozens of finished scripts, and every once in a while I would go through one to update it, but most of them sat idle. I had abandoned them, like a mother abandoning her babies.

Workless weeks like this stretched out before me and made me feel like a bum. I started drinking more heavily and smoking more weed, justifying it by saying I was an artist, so I was expected to drink during the day. I was on an unintended hiatus; I caught up with friends and tried to not think about anything work related. Unfortunately, I lived in LA, where the first question anyone asks is, "So, what are you working on now?"

"Not much" was the only answer I had. I hadn't worked on a movie in months, and I hadn't been shooting video on the side either. To my surprise, I actually missed shooting things myself. It was then I decided to buy a cinema camera and shoot something. Anything.

With Michael Madsen, on the set of Devil's Domain.

Wishing for a Dream (2017)

B lack Magic, a major camera company had announced its first pocket-sized cinema camera, and I was blown away by the image quality. The price was incredible, and I got to be one of the first people to buy one.

I was like a kid who'd gotten a new toy. The camera was tiny, with a vintage-inspired image capture similar to super 16 film—focused with a soft, nostalgic quality to it. My father lent me his vintage Nikkor lenses to try, and between the lenses and my camera, everything looked gorgeous. I had never been able to achieve such cinematic quality without a crew before.

I really wanted to put it to the test. Instead of shooting a camera test for YouTube, I decided to shoot a no-budget feature. It would be me, a few lights, my new camera, and a microphone. I was a crew of one.

I had no money for permits, but I had a camera that fit in my pocket, so I had the entire city as my location. At one point I even cut a hole in a small bag to poke the lens through so I could shoot in locations extra low-key—some real guerrilla shit.

The script was a semiautobiographical drama called *Wishing for a Dream*. It was about an actress, played by my then-fiancé Sara, and a director, played by me. The characters were trying to make it in Hollywood, very much like what we were doing in real life. It was a personal movie that came out as either a love or hate letter to the film industry, depending on how you look at it. It highlights what trying to make it actually looks like, very much like parts of this book.

I followed Sara around with the camera, stealing shots on Hollywood Boulevard. We got footage at auditions, the gym, the supermarket, and restaurants, showing her day-to-day as an actress on the grind. The production value was incredible. It was exciting to drive away from a restaurant after filming an entire scene with multiple setups and only have to pay the food tab.

It felt like I was back in New York, shooting wherever I wanted, stealing shots as if the world were free. I was taking a break from directing in Hollywood and going back to my roots, to a time when it was just me and my gear. It was liberating, and it reminded me that I can always create films by myself if I want to. Check it out at https://jaredcohn.com/movies/.

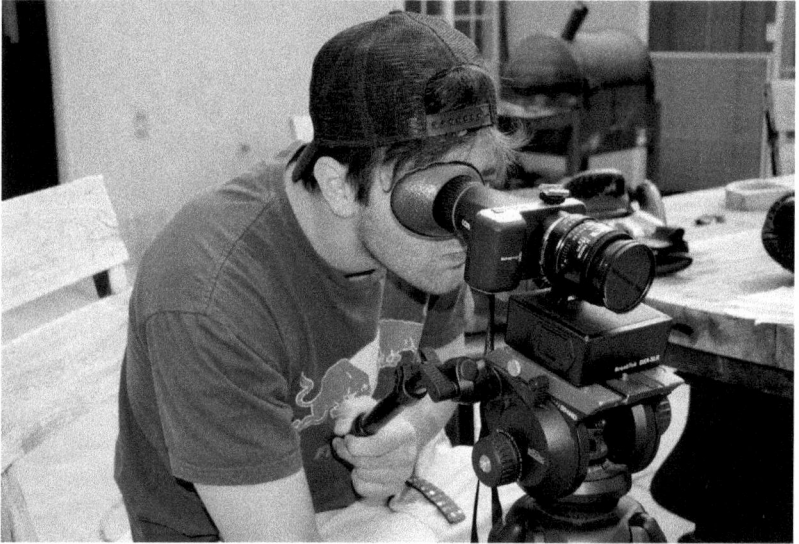

Shooting Wishing for a Dream on my Black Magic Pocket Camera.

Feed the Devil (2016)

Although I was fully committed to being a movie director, my dream of making it as an actor wasn't quite done with me.

Years prior, I had booked the lead role for a feature film shooting in Canada called *Feed the Devil*. The production kept being pushed back further and further until I assumed it was never going to happen. Then one day my phone rang. It was the production, calling to see if I was ready to head up north. Lucky for them, I wasn't working as a director at the time, so I was available.

The movie also happened to be shooting on 35 mm film, which is rare. Only big-budget movies are shot on film nowadays, and even then, most don't bother. With the exception of some art-house directors, only the majors like Tarantino and Christopher Nolan use film. It's sadly a dying medium, but I am confident someone will always keep it alive. You could compare shooting on film to listening to music on vinyl. It just feels more organic than digital does.

My role was a guy named Marcus who smokes, drinks, and gets killed by a demon midway through the movie. It'd take twenty days to shoot my part. I wasn't in bad shape, but I wasn't where I was when I was pursuing acting, so I started working out and dieting. That fear was all it took for my anxieties as an actor to come back. I didn't want to suck or look fat, and I had quite a few lines to learn. Running and push-ups became my religion, and I restricted my eating to cans of tuna.

After landing in Montreal, I met up with the director and his wife and drove four hours north to the middle of nowhere, otherwise known as Saint-Zenon. It was me, a couple of other actors, some crew, and the director staying at this snowy chalet where everyone spoke French.

Shortly after setting up, it became clear just how low-budget the shoot would actually be. There was no stunt coordinator despite the script calling for quite a few dangerous maneuvers. Some actors might have freaked out, but part of me liked being rebellious since we'd never get away with this type of thing in LA. So when the script called for a demon to leap on me, a PA in makeup climbed up a tree, and when the director, Max Perrier, called action, I just prayed the PA didn't land on my neck and paralyze me.

By the end, I had swum through a frozen lake, sprinted full speed into a ditch, gotten chased by a real wolf, and been sent down a white-water rapid with my hands tied behind my back. The experience reminded me of what exactly I asked actors to do on my movie sets. Stunts ask a lot from a performer, and this was a fun reminder of that.

While I was lucky not to get hurt during the stunts, what did hurt was getting crucified on a giant wooden cross. My arms were stretched out and tied up with rope for what felt like hours. By the time my character broke free and escaped, my shoulders were crackling. That pain lingered for days, but I didn't complain. I knew the production was maxed out on what they could handle, so I tried to be as easy to work with as possible. I was down to do whatever I could to help, and if that meant doing some crazy shit, there was no need to ask twice.

Revisiting the experience of being an actor and willfully doing crazy shit helps me communicate with actors when a scene calls for difficult action. As a director, I would never ask an actor to do something I wasn't willing to do myself. In fact, I wouldn't ask an actor to do half the shit I was willing to do myself.

Max Perrier was very picky about his shots, so it didn't take long before we were falling behind schedule quite a bit. I was supposed to get killed halfway into the movie, and then the lead woman, played by Ardis Barrow, would continue fighting and save the day. However, after running ten days past schedule with the movie still unfinished, Ardis decided she'd had enough and went back to New York. So did the rest of us, leaving *Feed the Devil* stamped with a giant question mark.

I went back to business as usual in LA and told myself it wouldn't finish. It was upsetting, but I wasn't trying to be an actor anyway, so I was off to find a movie to direct.

Over a year passed before Max Perrier called me, saying he wanted to finish the movie. In the interim, I had directed a few movies, but *Feed the Devil* had been part of my life since I was back at my dad's apartment in Long Island. I couldn't let it go.

Max asked me if I wanted to take over the main role and finish it out. He also let me know production had run out of money, so it would be unpaid work. I was hoping Ardis would go back to finish the movie so I wouldn't be in this predicament, but as a director myself, I understood wanting to complete your movie. Max said he would need another twenty days and that my character would not get killed, even though we already filmed my death scene. A new scene would be added where I survive, and Ardis's character dies instead. It seemed like the only option on the table if I wanted to finish the movie. But another twenty days in Canada for no pay—that was something to think about.

Max had shown me a couple of clips, and the movie looked beautiful on the developed 35 mm film. Of course it did—it was shot with vintage Russian Lomo anamorphic lenses. This was a tough spot to be in, but I could tell Max really wanted to finish this movie, so I agreed to go back to Canada. I remembered when my directorial debut was held up, it was awful. I wouldn't wish that on anyone. Max had trusted me enough to cast me, so I felt I should trust him enough to finish the movie.

I would be there much longer than anticipated: almost six weeks instead of twenty days.

The conditions weren't the best, and the crew was tiny, but this was real filmmaking. There were no permits, but I was down to make it work. I started having fun and improvising. Because I was starting to go crazy for real, it was reflected in my acting. I was on edge, and my performance was grittier because I was either cold, hot, or mosquito bitten.

Around day sixty, I started losing my mind. At one point, in between shots of me fighting demons, I was sitting on a dirt mound, covered in mud, and trying to swat away flies and mosquitos. It was futile; there were too many, and they didn't stop. I surrendered. They could have my blood.

For one scene, my character escapes in an old pickup truck, and Max wanted to film through the front window as I raced away from a demonic kill squad. Normally you'd rig the camera to the hood or put the vehicle on a process trailer driven by someone else, but not on this show. Max lay down on the hood of the pickup truck, grabbed on to the edge with one hand, and held a giant film camera on his shoulder with the other. In no uncertain terms, he ordered me to "speed off." A normal actor might've found it too dangerous, but I knew if I went slow, Max would yell at me for wasting film. I don't know how he held on as I accelerated down that rocky dirt road, but he did. For a tall, skinny guy, Max Perrier is Abe Lincoln strong.

There was a lot to learn from watching Max's directing style. The man is meticulous about every frame. Since he was shooting on film, he would not roll the camera until a shot was exactly how he wanted it. He would wait for the sun, he would wait for the clouds, he would wait out the rain if he had to. It made me think about my style and how fast I had to move. Unfortunately, I did not have the luxury of waiting like Max. On a nine-day shoot, when you have fifteen-plus pages to get through, you have to keep moving, or you will be replaced. One day, I thought.

At the end of the *Feed the Devil* script, my character kills the demon by bashing in its skull while burning down the shack they're in. Just as the shack is about to collapse, my character escapes with his life.

For the shot, Max entered the wood shack with a can of gas and a lighter and started dousing the place with me in it. Gas droplets splashed onto my skin, but after being stuck in Canada for over two months, I didn't care if I burned or not. He pulled out a lighter and lit the joint up, and *whoosh!* It got hot fast, my skin was literally cooking, and the roar of the fire encircling me was only intensifying. Max ran to the camera, waiting for the fire to look right. Meanwhile, I just waited for the word, and when he called action, I rushed out as the place crumbled behind me. It was a sick shot, and Max was way braver than I had ever been. I thought I was willing to do some crazy shit for a movie, but Max had me beat by a mile. There was no way I would ever get away with making a movie like that in LA. Hollywood is super safety conscious, which is not a bad thing. Max's style is how movies used to be made before all the safety rules came into place. Times have changed, but not for Max Perrier, and I was loving it.

Feed the Devil turned out well, and I really thought it might be my ticket to making a name for myself as an actor. I thought I looked great, and my performance was super solid. I was and still am proud of this movie, so I spent my own money to throw a big premiere in Hollywood in hopes the talent agents I invited would show up. Spoiler alert: they didn't.

I wanted to be like Clint Eastwood or Ben Affleck, directors who also have legit acting careers, filmmakers who can get a project greenlit and then go on to star in someone else's movie.

One of the main reasons filmmakers and actors want success is the luxury of options. When you are starting out, you have to take what is offered. You have no other choice. You could just say no and hope for something perfect, but I don't like hope. It hasn't favored me.

Despite my best efforts, *Feed the Devil* was not my *Good Will Hunting*. I was no Ben Affleck. It did not win Sundance. It went where most other movies go: to the all-welcoming ether.

I should also say that movie premieres, for the most part, are totally unnecessary. They're a vanity play that makes you feel good for the night, but they are also expensive. There's a big difference between the production company paying for a premiere and you footing the bill. When it's your money, you really think about how much the red-carpet photos are worth and whether you should get the cheap champagne or Trader Joe's red wine. Cheese plates add up. But again, after the hard work of making a movie, you should celebrate. The premiere was fun, but other than a cool Instagram story, it was worthless.

My acting career didn't work out the first time I was in LA, and it also didn't work the second time. At least I still had a little bit of a directing career, I told myself.

What I hadn't expected next was to hear from an old acquaintance. Years ago, on the very first Asylum movie I was cast in, I acted alongside Paul Logan, and he came to me with a very interesting proposal.

Starring in Feed the Devil, alongside Ardis Barrow, in Canada.

The Horde (2016)

⁓⁓⁓

Paul Logan is a muscle-bound, talented actor-writer-producer, and we both were in a movie called *The Way of the Vampire*. After that, we bumped into each other periodically over the years.

On one of these run-ins, he told me about a script he'd written called *The Horde*, and he thought I'd be a good candidate to direct while he took the lead role. When someone says they want you to direct their movie, it feels good. But in Hollywood, people say a lot of things, and those things usually don't come to fruition. Paul, however, was not messing around. The project wasn't just real. It was already financed.

Paul sent over the script, and I was impressed with it. His writing style was similar to mine, economical with words and straight to the point. The script consisted of Paul's character, an ex-Special Forces operative, taking on an army of mutant killers. It was action packed yet character driven. After working out a deal, I was all in.

Paul and I did some of the best prep work I've ever done on a movie because we had the time to do it. We spent almost two months selecting the best locations and getting all the blocking and fight choreography dialed in. On low-budget movies, you're usually under the gun with casting by the time you get to scouting, and you have no time to block things out until principal photography starts.

With locations nailed down, we went about assembling a cast of high school students to get killed off by the story's murderous mutants. We looked at a lot of girls, but one of the tapes stood out among the rest: that of then-seventeen-year-old Sydney Sweeney, giving an emotionally charged audition. We knew she would be perfect for the lead role, Hailey Summers. Sydney would quickly go on to be a megastar, landing a breakout lead role in HBO's *Euphoria*, among many other prestigious movies and shows. It's amazing to see the level of success she has achieved.

Alongside Sydney, we had Vernon Wells, Costas Mandylor, Don "the Dragon" Wilson, Bill Moseley, and Matt Willig—a legit cast of horror icons and star actors.

Despite this being a low-budget movie, we wanted it to look as expensive as possible. Every day during prep, Paul and I would see how far we could push things. We'd run through choreography just to see what else we could add. This dedication meant we were able to achieve a lot more than if we'd left it to the day of.

The movie had flaming arrows shot from rooftops, a guy on fire, and stuntmen flying out of moving vehicles as Paul was beating them down. All the heavy action had to be thoughtfully planned out with our stunt coordinator, Tony Snegoff, whom I would find myself working with quite a bit. Working with Tony is great because he understands my desire to push the envelope when it comes to action. Stunts can be dangerous, but there are safe ways to get them done, and that's what good stunt coordinators do. *The Horde* turned out fantastic, and Paul threw an amazing premiere for it. If *The Horde 2* is ever made, hopefully it's big budget enough for Sydney Sweeney to return. (That said, she's probably about to win an Oscar as I type this.) While she went on to superstardom, I unfortunately did not. It was back to the grind as usual.

On location, directing The Horde, with stars Paul Logan and Sydney Sweeney.

Evil Nanny (2016)

L ong live The Asylum! I'll say it all day. They put me on the map
with *Born Bad*, so they will forever have a spot in my heart.
When they call, I answer. And they called. The movie they pitched
was about a psycho nanny and about as Lifetime as it gets, but the
script was written by longtime collaborator Naomi Selfman. They
didn't need to say more.

Evil Nanny is about, well, an evil nanny, but one who battles against
a young mother. We cast two fantastic actresses for the main roles,
but there was an issue: they both had dark hair. With a better
understanding of color story under my belt, I wanted to create
contrast. Two dark-haired women fighting each other at night
wouldn't read well on screen; they'd be hard to tell apart. I wanted
the nanny's hair to be blonde, a sharp departure from the mom's
dark hair. Lindsay Elston, the actress playing the evil nanny, got her
hair dyed.

When I saw a photo of the new hair color, I was in full prep mode,
making a dozen daily decisions leading up to the shoot. I thought
she looked great and moved on to the next thing. However, day one
of the shoot arrives, and we shoot the first scene. An hour later, my
phone begins ringing aggressively, and I knew I'd fucked up. It turns
out that begging for forgiveness was not better than asking for
permission.

When the producers saw the change, it was an immediate summons
to their office. That meant I would have to leave set to go to the
production office even though it was downtown LA and the middle

168

of the day. I knew I was in for a tongue-lashing, but most of all, I didn't want to leave the set. I blocked out a scene and gave as clear instructions as I could before venturing off.

Taking a car would be a disaster; there was way too much traffic. Thankfully, Harwood Gordon, the most badass guy around, was on set. Harwood was a seventy-year-old guy with a white beard, six-pack abs, and a motorcycle. I asked him if he could spin me to The Asylum in the fastest, most dangerous way possible. After explaining the situation further, he understood the urgency. The problem was he didn't have a spare helmet, and it was illegal to not wear one. In a pinch, I used black gaff tape to cover the shit out of my baseball cap in hopes a passing cop wouldn't notice.

When I got off outside the office and took a deep breath, it hit me that I could get fired over this. Maybe the producers were so upset they'd had enough. I paused before entering The Asylum, which now felt scarier than ever, and took my seat before the serious-looking producers. As predicted, I got chewed out for not getting permission to dye the hair. They were right to be mad. The cast approval process is no joke, and I had changed the equation. All three partners have to sign off on the lead roles, and all three had signed off on two brunettes, so they were expecting to see two brunettes.

I was trying to create contrast, but I hadn't realized that a blonde-haired character might be interpreted differently than a brunette. Maybe there were implications beyond my understanding, or maybe a buyer had a thing against blonde hair. I don't know. What I do know is that I made a visual change without clearing it with the higher-ups. While I didn't get fired, I never again changed an actor's look without discussing it with people financing the picture. I left that meeting feeling awful, like a kid who drew in somebody else's notepad in class.

Getting back to the set snapped me out of my self-loathing, and I got back to work. I had a job to do, and I was going to do it. The hair wasn't changing back, and there would be no money for reshoots, so the blonde hair would stay. Even though I failed to get permission, making bold decisions is ultimately part of what makes a director's style. A lot of directors wouldn't have thought about doing what I did, but it was a choice, and one that changed it up.

The hair wasn't the only stamp I put on the film. Our climactic ending scene called for cops to swarm in and stop the crazy nanny from killing the mom. Because I was feeling extra militant and aggressive instead of guilty at this point, I decided I wanted the police to be a SWAT team, complete with a sniper. I wanted them to storm in violently—I was tired of using the same old Crown Victoria police cars that every low-budget movie used. I wanted imposing SUVS like you'd see in real life.

I directed the cops to not smile and treat the mom as though she was a suspect through the happy ending. This felt more realistic to the situation. I was angry, and this was how I dealt with it. I demanded my vision. The cops would not enter with handguns but with AR-15s and shotguns, which I was proud of. People may not remember or talk about it, but details like that made the whole scene feel more intense. The end of the movie was a hostage situation with an armed suspect, and I felt this tactical approach was warranted. I liked playing with toy guns when I was a kid, and that didn't change in adulthood. As long as you can make a valid argument for something as a director, you should go for it. Do enough of these things, and your overall style starts to feel different, more personal.

Heavily armed police, on set of Evil Nanny.

King Arthur (2017)

B y 2017, I was on a roll and happy to be rolling. I didn't want it to stop, but I also knew that it could end at any moment. The *Evil Nanny* edit had finished at The Asylum, and I was now on the hunt for my next project.

Anna Rasmussen worked on the development team at The Asylum at the time, and I often bothered the shit out of her to check up on the slate of upcoming movies. She was kind enough to keep me up to date, and I would always ask if there was a director attached when I came across something interesting.

One upcoming project was simply called the King Arthur movie, which had a completed script. In addition to the expected sword fighting, this version was filled with magic and time travel that culminated in a giant robot smashing the city. Intrigued, I asked Anna to send me the script.

It was written by my talented friend Scotty Mullen and was full of fast-paced action from start to finish. I marched into the executive office to throw my hat in the ring to direct. The ink on *Evil Nanny* had barely dried, yet there I was, asking for another job. It felt greedy, like maybe I should let someone else have it, but with no other income, I needed to keep going. Especially if I didn't want to start shooting videos again.

Now, just because I had a decent track record didn't mean I'd get the job. The Asylum has a talented roster of directors, and when something interesting comes along, they fight for it. Luckily, I had an edge.

Like I said, Scotty Mullen was a good friend. I pitched Scotty my vision for the film with as much spectacle as I could, and he thankfully had my back. I was then given the golden nod by the producers, David Latt, Paul Bales, and David Rimawi, and the King Arthur movie was mine for the taking. No matter how many movies I do, getting the job will always be a good feeling.

The script called for all sorts of unique and fantastical locations, so the idea of not shooting in LA came up early on. This sent my wheels spinning; it was an opportunity to go anywhere in the world to make a movie. Where would I want to go?

A couple of years prior, Sara and I performed in a horror movie in Thailand called *Pernicious*, which my friend James Cullen Bressack wrote and directed. The locations were stunning and staggeringly different from anything in North America. With the option to choose where to shoot this futuristic take on King Arthur, Thailand became an immediate, interesting choice.

Convincing a producer to take a show abroad is a big ask, so I wanted to make sure my argument for doing a King Arthur movie in Thailand didn't sound moronic. I reached out to the producer from *Pernicious*, Daemon Hillin, a savvy guy with offices in LA and Bangkok, to tell him about my plan. Daemon put together a comprehensive presentation of available exotic locations, and we constructed a valid argument for why Thailand would work for the film.

With the labor costs and the location fees significantly lower in Thailand than in LA, it wasn't a difficult equation, even when factoring in travel and lodging.

I'm sure Michael Bay stays at the Ritz Carlton when he travels. We, on the other hand, stayed at a seedy hotel in the middle of Bangkok's red-light district, where the streets were filled with prostitutes pulling on us, calling out for business. Not my kind of party, but there was no shortage of expats enjoying their retirement.

Filmmaking in Thailand is different. Crews work differently, with entirely different positions than we see in the United States. For instance, they had a crew member assigned to a single light, and that was it. Because of tight roles like that, we had a large crew of over fifty people.

Our Thai crew worked hard and nonstop. The concept of breaking for lunch was our American thing; they would eat while they worked. They would climb up poles to set lights and then chain-smoke while practicing Muay Thai with each other during their free time. These guys were insanely badass. I've never seen anything like it.

I had a pimped-out mobile video village team with giant monitors and a full PA system, not a megaphone, that I could use to communicate across the set. I felt like a big-time movie director there.

It's fun directing a huge crew. You feel like a general at war, giving orders and watching people carry them out. Thankfully nobody was dying on my set. We were making art in Thailand, and thanks to Daemon, we had access. We shut down streets and filmed wherever we wanted, all with police protection. The world of weird bureaucratic permissions was gone, and we were able to shoot and do stunts in a city subway station. In the States, that kind of access is only granted to major studios that can afford it.

My then-fiancé Sara Malakul Lane was cast to play the evil lead, Morgana. Sara grew up in Thailand and both modeled and starred on the screen. She's super famous there, constantly appearing in tabloids and magazines and on billboards. Walking around Bangkok with her was like walking around with Sydney Sweeney in LA. Fans stopped her left and right to ask for pictures. I knew she was famous before we went, but seeing it in person was a different story. I was impressed by her stardom, but she was used to it and always was super kind to her fans. It was wonderful to see her there being celebrated. I was proud of her. She had left such a high level of celebrity, the ability to work in whatever TV and movies she wanted, to try and make it in Hollywood.

During the shoot, Sara had a full press conference with about fifty reporters in attendance. When I was asked a question at her side, it was more cameras and mics than I'd ever seen. It was like I was Sam Raimi at a Comic-Con panel. I was featured in Thai gossip magazines and even found my face plastered on a giant wall. It was quite an interesting adventure. Directing abroad is amazing. The American way is not the only way films are made, and I feel a lot can be learned from other countries.

Shooting King Arthur on the streets of Thailand with Producer Daemon Hillin and DP Josh Maas.

Press conference with Sara Malakul Lane while shooting King Arthur in Thailand.

Back on It

B ack to La-La Land. Time passes differently in LA. I look at my watch, and it's next week. Then it's been months, and you realize you haven't done shit. I bugged Anna in development again at The Asylum, but all of the upcoming projects either already had directors or were far in the future.

Jailbait, a movie I'd done with Sara a few years back, had done well, so I came up with the idea to pitch *Jailbait 2* to the producers, who were receptive. Receptive is good. So I wrote an outline and sent it in. I just assumed if I kept nudging them, I could make the movie happen.

"Kindly checking in. Did Rimawi read the *Jailbait 2* outline? I look forward to hearing his thoughts!"

I was polite yet enthusiastically to the point.

This can be called persistence or annoyance, and I was definitely toeing the line. But without a movie to direct, what the hell else could I do? After a couple of weeks, the producers called and asked me to come to the office.

When I entered Rimawi's office, I learned he hadn't read the outline but intended to read it right there in front of me. Gulp. As he did, he would occasionally pause, look up from the page, and think. Meanwhile, my anxious brain was ping-ponging all over the place. Was he trying to figure out how to tell me it sucked? Did he love it? He put the paper down and paused again. After what felt like an eternity, he said he enjoyed it. What a relief! He gave me some notes to improve the main character and to make the evil one more evil, but he ultimately gave me the green light to move on and write the eight-act treatment. The *Jailbait 2* wheels were officially in motion.

To write a detailed eight-act treatment for a feature-length movie, your plot needs to be fully developed, and the characters need to be fairly fleshed out. There is a big difference between coming up with an idea for a movie and then actually writing it out, creating the characters, and coming up with a beginning, middle, and end. The outline phase is probably harder than actually writing the script for me because the outline is where you have to come up with everything. After that, writing the script is easy. You just follow the outline and hope the voices in your head lead to decent dialogue.

After days of writing and rewriting, I had a few pages about a troubled girl who finds herself in a corrupt jail with an underground fighting ring. It had suicide, rape, death, sex, fights, and a jailbreak to top it off. It was extra gritty, but I liked it, so off it went. After the requisite waiting period, I got notes from development that I promptly addressed before resubmitting and waiting. Again. As you can see, waiting is a big part of the game, and not just on the set.

Writing movies and pushing projects along requires vast amounts of patience. To be honest, I hate waiting, but when you're the writer, there's only so much you can do to expedite things. Sometimes the only and best thing to do is sit back, shut up, and wait.

After a week or two, I was happy to be informed the waiting game was over, and that my eight-act treatment was approved.

Back to my computer all over again. The outline for *Jailbait 2* was taped to my wall, but now a blank page in a file called "Final Draft" was staring back at me. I wanted this script to be great, so I dug in and started clacking away at the keys.

I wanted to go dark with the tone, so to get into a heady space, I drank whiskey, smoked weed, and listened to industrial music while writing for days. I went old school. When you commit to just sitting down and writing, wonderful things happen. I enforced rules like not allowing myself to stand up, remove my wrists from the laptop, or do anything else but write. There is a natural inclination to procrastinate, and this resistance must be defeated to successfully complete a draft.

Between my lack of sleep, my blasting angry music, and the drinking, I was an irritable, agitated mess. Because of this, the dialogue I wrote became more cutting; the characters were a little colder, and the tone became petulant. The entire feel of a story can be affected by the author's headspace. I don't recommend getting fucked up to write, but if you know what you are doing, sometimes it helps.

When I was done, I stared at the finished one hundred pages of words. When you complete the first draft, you think magic fairies are going to burst out and sprinkle you with pixie dust. That never happens. Instead you usually just have a headache. It is less a feeling of elation and more a sense of relief. The way I wrote was hardcore, intense. It was hours of typing without stopping. After completing a draft, I could finally take a breath.

Following another round of notes and revisions, the script was set, and the conversation changed to how we were actually going to make it. It was in one of these meetings that David Latt laid out the budget and said we didn't have to shoot in LA if we could find an alternative. That sounded like a reason to go back to Thailand to me. I had a great time before, and getting out of LA sounded good.

Of course, I would have to rewrite the script to be set in Thailand, but that was fine. Nobody likes having to do extra work, but no script ever fits the locations perfectly. Most of the time, some tweaking is necessary to accommodate the layout of the house that's booked or something like that. However, when your script changes continents, you have a bit more typing to do. Thankfully, I knew how to type.

Casting this movie was going to be a challenge because the main role required a lot of grit. In addition to nudity, the lead would have to fight other girls, get gang-raped, and be beaten up. It was a gnarly story, and we didn't have many days to make it work. It was a tall order all around.

With the date to fly to Thailand fast approaching, we still hadn't cast our lead actress. We decided to hold one more round of auditions at the last second in the hopes we could find our star. Otherwise, the entire shoot would have to get pushed, and when a shoot gets pushed, there's always a chance it gets pushed off a cliff.

Toward the end of the casting session, I was getting bummed. Every girl we saw just wasn't it, and I was sure the movie would get pushed indefinitely. I was mad at myself for writing a script that was just too gnarly to cast.

And then in walked Kelly McCart, a fresh-faced, red-haired girl. She looked innocent, like a girl who didn't belong in jail, which was exactly what we wanted for our fish-out-of-water story. She crushed the audition. Not only did she have the look, but she also had the chops. The question was, how cool was she going to be with all the craziness in the script? She said it would be no problem, but I asked her to read the whole thing and let me know what she thought. I needed Kelly to say yes, or else I wasn't going to Thailand anytime soon.

Later that day, she got back to me and said the nudity and everything else would be no problem at all. I first thought her cavalier attitude was too good to be true, but it turns out she was just an absolute trooper, which made my job way easier. Having actors that are enthusiastic and happy to be there is a million times better than working with grumpy performers. Especially when that grumpy performer is a lead that complains every time they have to do something. That just makes everyone else just as miserable. Needless to say, I was grateful for Kelly's awesome attitude.

We waited to cast the rest of the roles until we landed in Bangkok. These would be the other inmates and the big supporting role of the mother. While the talent pool might not be as vast as it is in Los Angeles, there are definitely some talented actresses living in Bangkok.

The role of the mother was big, as the character would try to get her daughter out of jail, visit, and go to court. Numerous important scenes hinged on this actress despite her only filming for four days. We held auditions at the production offices, cast a talented local actress, and set up to film her the following day.

At the crack of dawn, production got an emergency call from the actress playing the mother. Her appendix had burst. But what surprised me even more than the emergency was that the partners' solution was to approve me as her replacement. They wanted me to act in the movie I was directing.

At this point, I didn't want to compromise the movie by splitting my attention. I resisted, asking if they could find anyone else to play the part, but the answer was a hard no. That meant I would also have to rewrite it because I was too young to have a teen daughter. I would have to become an uncle who happened to live in Thailand.

This much change at once threw a monkey wrench into my mind. I was so stressed that I bummed a cigarette from one of the crewmates even though I don't smoke. At that moment I needed something, and that Thai cigarette was delicious. The funny thing was, not too long ago, I would've killed for the opportunity to play a big role in a movie shooting in Thailand. I decided that with no choice but to play the part, I was going all in, and I wanted to look cool. Gotta look cool.

I swapped the backstory to where, instead of teaching English overseas like the mother, my character was an ex-drug-trafficker-turned-arms-dealer, living it up in a baller mansion in Thailand. I insisted on my character having three cell phones because a guy doing all sorts of shady international business would, of course, need at least three phones and a different chunky gold watch for every scene. I was suddenly very particular about this character's look because I hadn't been able to plan it, so I had to make important decisions on the spot.

I sent the wardrobe people out to scramble for knock-off designer clothes that I would take home with me. If I was going to do this, I wanted to at least walk away with some new gear. It took the Thai wardrobe costumer a few shopping trips to find clothes I approved of. I guess telling them I want to look like Justin Timberlake didn't quite translate. So there I was, standing in my boxers, getting fitted by the wardrobe people when I wasn't directing scenes. I felt bloated looking at myself in the mirror, wishing I had known I was about to be on camera. I definitely would've worked out and dieted a bit.

When the time came for my first scene as an actor, I put on the clothes, shaved, got into hair and makeup, and looked in the mirror again. I was no longer in my baggy cargo shorts, wrinkled T-shirt, and backward hat. I wasn't Jared Cohn the director; I was Uncle Tommy, rocking Gucci, three cell phones, and a baller mansion.

Although I had to get my scenes done fast, I didn't want to suck as an actor. I took a moment to get into character before calling for the cameras to roll. I made someone else call action and then started saying lines. I think I did all right. Well, at least there was nobody there to tell me I sucked if I did since I was the director.

Kelly and I did scenes at the jail and the courtroom. I pleaded to a Thai judge to spare my niece from getting tossed into jail, but Uncle Tommy failed, and she was locked away.

We filmed all over. Including at a Thai university and on some beautiful docks on the river where Kelly gets even with a bully by whacking her in the face with a board. The scenery and locations in Thailand are indescribably beautiful.

One night after shooting, I was too hungry to diet and too tired to walk the short distance to the 7-Eleven to get my usual ham and cheese sandwich. Lucky for me, there were rows and rows of street food vendors just outside my hotel. Some were scarier than others, with freshly slaughtered animals on display, but some of them looked pretty good.

I'm a basic eater, hence my 7-Eleven dinners, but I was so hungry I was willing to try some street food. I ordered the most basic-looking chicken dish I saw, gobbled it up, and went up to my dilapidated hotel room in the red-light district. I set my alarm and lay down to go to sleep. As soon as I closed my eyes, my stomach started gurgling. Seconds later, the sweating started. I got right out of bed and ran straight to the bathroom as the pain rocketed from zero to ten.

I tried to puke, tried to shit—anything to get the street food out of me. But nothing happened. Delirious, I stumbled to a local pharmacy and swallowed a bunch of laxatives in desperation. I was drenched in cold sweat, and the pain was still somehow worsening.

I sat on a toilet in my room, garbage can in hand, shoving my fingers down my throat, trying to purge any way I could. At a certain point, my skin went white, my lips started swelling, and the hallucinations started. I saw pulsing lights and felt like I was melting while sweating like I was in a sauna with a winter coat on. In a haze, I searched for a nearby hospital and piled myself into a taxi. It was already past midnight, and I had to be ready for pickups at 6:00 a.m. I hoped they could fix me up quickly so I could get some sleep. The most important thing to me was that I didn't miss pickups. But I was pretty fucked up and in hella pain.

The hospital was nice, and the staff there was friendly. They prodded me, ran some tests, and told me I was severely food poisoned. They gave me some injections and pills and then an enema, blasting liquids through me to wash everything out. It was disgusting, but also a big relief.

I shivered in my hospital bed, my cold sweat beading while I kept an eye on the clock. It was almost 5:00 a.m., and I had to leave if I wanted to make the shuttle to the set. I hadn't slept all night and was extremely light-headed, but I insisted on being released. No way I was going to miss pickups. I had a movie to direct.

My shaky legs barely held me as I pulled off whatever was taped onto me. I checked the mirror—I looked like a drug addict who'd been on a weeklong bender. I slapped my cheeks and splashed cold water on my face to get it together. Not sleeping sucks, but after not sleeping at all on *Hold Your Breath,* one sleepless night would be an easy obstacle.

I signed a liability release and rushed out, caught a taxi, and went right to the pickup location in time for the shuttle. A few minutes into the road, I was trembling, nauseous beyond belief, and my body started gurgling loudly. The location was a forty-five-minute drive away, and I had to purge from both ends. I simply kept my head down, bit my lip, and grimaced, hoping I wasn't going to shit my shorts. I didn't want to tell anyone about my fiasco.

As soon as we got to the location, I sprinted to the closest bathroom I could find. What came out was a bloody mess. I freaked out, wondering what the hell I'd been injected with. I didn't have time to bleed. Ten minutes later, my stomach started up again. I don't know what the Thai hospital put in me, but whatever it was, it wanted back out. I tried not to think about the blood as it came out, hoping I wasn't dying.

I was standing on top of an abandoned mall doubling as a jail, directing about eighty people across the set. The inmates were supposed to be on work duty, so I had them scrubbing the concrete ground. I was checking the image, making sure it looked good, when it hit me again. The bathrooms were five long minutes away, down four flights of stairs, and around the building. I made that trip about a dozen times within a few hours, sprinting back and forth. At some point, my body just started leaking. It was bad. I would not be eating any more street food. After a few days, I healed up a bit, but it would be another week or so before I was back to normal.

When I'm directing a movie, I don't call in sick. Directors can't do that. Same for actors. Filmmaking isn't like working a shift at a restaurant; nobody is there to replace you. If you are the director or actor, you must find a way to arrive at the set—and on time. Unless you were hit by a truck or are literally dead, there's no taking the day off, and there's no whining about it. There's no crying in filmmaking. It's just the way it is.

The climactic fight of the movie was set on top of a high roof at night. I had spent time with our cast and the stunt coordinator to work out a fight sequence with a lot of punches, kicks, hair grabs, and throws. The action needed to look gritty and realistic.

The location had amazing 360-degree views high above Bangkok. With shots filtered through a chain-link fence and falling rain, everything felt that much more cinematic. The only problem was the possibility of lightning. Lightning is no good. When the team heard about the potential for lightning, some immediately suggested finding an alternate indoor location for the fights. Unfortunately, nowhere was nearly as cool as the rooftop, and we'd lose all the time it took to break down and reset elsewhere.

The Thai crew bravely set up lights in the rain and put bags over the cameras as the actors stepped onto the set. I called action, and bit by bit, the actors began going through the fight choreography. Kelly, our lead, was really bringing it. The rain picked up. Between shots, I heard more murmurs about potential lightning, but the weather apps couldn't agree on the probability. There was now a whole debate, but I needed to shoot.

Tensions were high as heavy rain poured down. Everyone was drenched, ponchos were handed out, and people were checking their weather apps and comparing forecasts. I was told numerous times that if lightning got close enough, we would have to move. The last thing I wanted was for anyone to get hurt, but I didn't want to move if we didn't have to. The Americans have a rule called the thirty-thirty rule: if thunder is heard within a certain number of seconds after you see lightning, it's too close. However, the Thai crew did not have any such rule in place. In fact, the Thai crew was not worried about the lightning at all.

I carried on filming in the rain, praying the lightning would not come too close to violate the thirty-thirty rule, and it didn't. All that worrying for nothing. The fight scenes looked awesome in the rain, and we now had an epic climax in the can. Sometimes things work out. You just might have to push to get what you want. That said, you also have to be sensitive to other people around you. You have the power when you're directing, but you shouldn't push when the crew isn't comfortable. We were lucky the lightning didn't get too close, and we were rewarded with slick footage. I'm glad I stuck to my guns and didn't just move for no reason.

After wrapping I took the long flight back to Los Angeles to get checked out by a doctor. Luckily there'd been no lasting damage from my culinary adventure. Next time, no more street food.

I was anxious when it was time to edit the scenes I was in. What if I was dog shit? Fortunately, the scenes worked really well, and I didn't totally suck. The backstory of my character worked, and most importantly, I thought I looked cool. I was happy.

The movie would not be released as *Jailbait 2* but rather as *Locked Up*. If you want to see me acting as an international arms dealer, tune in.

Kelly McCart and me on set, acting as her uncle, in Locked Up, in Thailand.

After School Special (2017)

B ack in LA, producing prodigy Richard Switzer called me up to tell me about a comedy project. It was one of the wackiest scripts I had ever seen, filled with raunchy humor, fart jokes, and a scene that called for hundreds of dildos hanging in a school hallway.

I had done a comedy before, but this was borderline slapstick. It was called *School's Out*, and Richard himself would be playing the lead role alongside comedy legend Nick Swardson. Jason London, David Chokachi, Eric Roberts, and porn stars Ron Jeremy and Kayden Kross were also signed on to perform. It was a star-studded cast of comedians, porn stars, and name actors.

During a preproduction lunch meeting with the department heads, we discussed our crew size. Since this was a low-budget shoot, we wanted to keep our crew relatively small. The original DP, a guy named Gus, decided the crew size we were considering wasn't sufficient for him. One of the producers tried to explain the budget and what we could afford, but Gus wasn't having it. He snapped at the producer, and right there in a West Hollywood restaurant, a full-on argument took place. DP Gus showed everyone he was short-tempered and unreasonable.

After that, I pulled one of the producers aside and voiced my concerns about keeping him on. I'd have to work closely and creatively with the DP, and I didn't want Gus. I warned producers that Gus wouldn't play well with others, but nobody wanted to go through the trouble of looking for a cinematographer last minute.

Just as I predicted, Gus started arguing with everybody on the set. I had never seen someone so disliked by everyone simply for having a bad attitude. I almost felt bad for the guy until we were shooting a scene in the backyard of a house. It was a simple shot. Our lead actors were sneaking into a party. We got a nice wide shot, showing the world, the big yard, and the party decorations, and then I called for a close-up to show the actors' faces. At this, Gus said, "We don't need a close-up. The wide shot was beautiful. It's all we need." Now I, like everyone else on the set, was not a fan of him. A director should never have to argue with a DP to get what he needs. I insisted on the shot but later told producers I never wanted to work with Gus again.

The same day, I overheard some of the actors talking about Gus. Apparently, he was trying to hook up with one of the actresses and asking her out during production. Really unprofessional stuff. The shoot, which was supposed to be a fun comedy, was not feeling fun at all. One bad apple definitely spoils the bunch. Every day Gus showed up, something bad happened.

After hearing about the girl, I was on my way to ask the producers to fire Gus when I overheard shouting. Gus was arguing with one of the production staff, but this wasn't just any argument. It was escalating. I heard the producer calling Gus a piece of shit, and I darted over to see the two of them screaming in each other's faces. I start calling for them both to calm down when the burly Gus decided a verbal assault wasn't enough and charged. They started throwing punches and kicks at each other. A full-on fight on my set!

Crewmembers rushed to break up the fight, and I told Gus that I was personally embarrassed for him. Finally, production fired him. I could not believe that actually happened.

It's important to hire the right people and make sure they play nicely together. When you're moving fast and crewing up a low-budget show, putting together a great team can be a challenge. The really great guys often work all the time and usually on high-budget, high-paying projects.

Sometimes the people you want are booked or unavailable for whatever reason, and you hire new people. Sometimes it works out great, and you work with that person for a long time; other times you hire them, and they start fistfights.

Directing Eric Roberts, Ron Jeremy and Richard Switzer in After School Special.

Halloween Pussy Trap Kill! Kill! (2017)

 decorative divider

I was at Cleopatra Record's office in west LA, drinking Jack Daniels with my friend Brian Perera. We'd made *Devil's Domain* together and were talking about doing another movie. Something he said about a rock band reminded me of a script I had written years prior during one of my weed- and alcohol-fueled writing binges. I had written so many scripts in various states of mental fuckery that sometimes I forgot about them, but I remembered that one.

My script was a *Saw*-esque horror plot about a mastermind who captures an all-girl rock band called Death House. At one point, years ago, I had optioned the script to a production company, so I knew the script was in good enough shape to pitch. I decided, what the hell, I'd shoot my shot and pitched it.

Brian read the script and said it was right up his alley. It was a smooth pitch-to-green-light scenario, and I was happy to have another movie to direct. Sometimes you have to go to pitch events and wait for months. Sometimes the movie gods line things up for you.

We brought on microbudget producer David Sterling and started crunching numbers, figuring out what this movie would actually cost to make. A lot can be learned from David Sterling's efforts to get things done for cheap. No permits, low pay, cheap food, and no negotiating. Sterling's ways aren't for everyone, but his unconventional methods work every time, which is why he's made over two hundred movies. Mixing some of his methods with ours benefited the bottom line tremendously.

We found a cast of beautiful, talented actresses to play the band, but Brian wanted some additional star power to help sales. As always, that was fine by me, so we brought in screen legend Richard Grieco to play the bad guy. I grew up watching Grieco on *21 Jump Street*, so it was really cool to have him with us.

While we were finalizing our cast, we were also location scouting. We found this old factory basement downtown that looked like an underground dungeon. It had thick concrete walls filled with manic scribblings like "There's no God here" and giant machines I'm sure did something important fifty years ago. Now they just made for interesting set design. This place, as it was, looked like a fully dressed set for one of the *Saw* movies. The air was a little musty, but I really wanted the location because nowhere else came close to its creepy uniqueness. Problem was, it was way more than we'd originally budgeted for.

We scouted out a few other locations, but my heart was set. The majority of the movie takes place at the mastermind's dungeon, and the downtown basement was too good to pass up. I dug in my heels and fought. I would have to sacrifice a full day of the shooting schedule to afford the location, but it was the right move. I had to shoot there.

Day one arrived, and the crew was lugging the film gear downstairs to the basement of the old building. I started hearing murmurs about the air quality and how it was hot as fuck down there. The heat and stale air didn't bother me, but just a few hours into filming the dungeon scenes, the cast and crew started complaining a lot. This would be a problem.

Production did all sorts of things to make the situation better like renting giant air purifiers, as well as a massive air-conditioning system—all of which were additional unexpected expenses, but necessary ones to protect the crew and cast. No matter what we did, though, it wasn't good enough. The air down there was bad. Even I was starting to breathe heavily.

Worse, we had to shoot a scene with all the actors locked in a room. The script called for poisonous gas to be blasted on them, so we were pumping in fog and setting off colored-smoke grenades on top of everything. I didn't really think of the logistics when I was stoned writing the script and coming up with interesting ways to torture people. It didn't take much to sell the cast's writhing on the floor as they pretended to choke on poisoned air.

Even as I started feeling the effects of the heat and the air, I couldn't leave the set except for lunch. I had to simply condition my body to accept it and power through. Once my adrenaline kicks in, I'm in the zone. After surviving the sleepless nights on *Hold Your Breath*, I knew I would be fine. That said, I still felt awful making everyone suffer by keeping them down there. But what could I do except continue making the movie? I couldn't just stop. The film must always be completed. Eventually we finished in the dungeon, took some deep breaths, and were fine. Nobody got hurt.

Since we were filming around Halloween, what better place to film than the Santa Monica Halloween Carnaval? It's an event with five hundred thousand revelers, DJs, rock bands, and food vendors. It's like Times Square on New Year's Eve. Having our actors there would add massive production value, so despite not having a permit, we marched forward. We figured there would be way too much going on for the cops to care about us doing a little filming on a giant Arri Alexa cinema camera. We were right.

Drones were becoming popular, and I decided I wanted some aerial shots of the parade in addition to footage of the girls partying. We realized that the likelihood of getting a permit to fly over people at one of the busiest events in West Hollywood was nil, so we decided to roll the dice and see if we could do it without going to jail.

We booked a hotel room located at the start of the parade and the pilot sent up the drone. Party people flagged the drone from below, gawking and pointing at it. The pilot landed it right as I saw an LAPD officer point at it. We freaked out and rushed inside the cramped hotel room to hide for a bit. Thankfully no cops knocked on the door, and upon reviewing the footage we had a really slick ten-second clip that made it into the movie. It was all worth it for that one shot. You have to do what you have to do to get cool shots as long as nobody gets hurt.

After we got the drone footage, it was time to take our massive cinema camera onto the streets. I was worried about getting stopped by the police, but there were so many people, nobody cared we were filming. The cops were way too busy dealing with crowds of drunken, naked, or just plain high people to care about us. It was debauchery and revelry at the highest level at this parade. It would've cost way too much to pay for these shots.

During postproduction, Dave Mustaine, lead singer of Megadeth and original member of Metallica, was brought on to voice the mastermind. I flew to Nashville to direct him at a recording studio before I went about spending the next few days enjoying the city. There were bars with loud live music, where I hung out and got drunk with the locals. Then it was back to LA, back on the grind.

When I wrote the script for the horror movie, I titled it *Death House*, but another *Death House* was being made by the time we started. To change things up, it was shot under the name *Halloween Hell House*. However, when it came time to release it, it was put out as *Halloween Pussy Trap Kill! Kill!* as an homage to Russ Meyer's classic, *Faster, Pussycat! Kill! Kill!* I received a couple of grievances from the cast about the name change, as I don't think they wanted the word *pussy* anywhere near their IMDb page. Nonetheless, title changes happen all the time, and as the hired writer-director, I didn't have a say.

Halloween Pussy Trap Kill! Kill! Was a good experience, but it was no bigger or splashier than anything else I was doing. To be honest, I wasn't super excited to have another one of my movies premiere, only to see it drift into the ether. It's disappointing, but that's exactly what happened.

On Location with Richard Grieco and Demetrius Stear, and crew for Halloween Pussytrap Kill! Kill!

Atlantic Rim 2 (2018)

I had pretty much given up on updating my director demo reel and reaching out to agents. They weren't interested in me before because I had done too many low-budget movies, so why would they be interested after I'd done even more? I always try and make the best thing I can with the resources I have, but continually being disappointed with where you're at in life can be exhausting.

At least I was working, I told myself. I had many peers who weren't working as much or at all, so I tried to be grateful for what I had. On the flip side, I also knew people who were signed by the Creative Artists Agency or WME, had their films in Sundance, and were supremely successful. I tried not to be jealous.

One day while reading *The Hollywood Reporter*, I saw Guillermo del Toro was back at it again, making *Pacific Rim 2*. Well, I had directed *Atlantic Rim*, and it did well. Pitching The Asylum on *Atlantic Rim 2* seemed like a logical play if I wanted to keep surviving on making movies.

I drafted an email with information about *Pacific Rim 2*'s release date, but it turned out I was pitching something already on their slate. Luckily, I hadn't messed up too much with the first one, so they were kind enough to keep me around.

The budget for *Atlantic Rim 2* was less than the original, and the schedules kept getting shorter. We had fifteen days to shoot the first one, and now we were down to nine for the entire movie. The market had changed. More movies were and are being made by more people. With more supply, there's less demand, and yesterday's price isn't today's. People can now afford to buy 4K cameras and shoot full-length movies on their own. The playing field was leveled, and that meant more competition, tighter budgets, and shorter schedules to stay competitive.

Moving at a faster pace means less time and more stress. If one thing doesn't work, it can really mess you up. For instance, the sci-fi glasses we used for the actors as they fought sea creatures from inside their robot cockpits kept getting knocked askew. Our passionate young actors were throwing themselves around violently, and these glasses kept falling off their faces. It was frustrating because if they weren't worn perfectly, they looked silly and ruined the shot. We had to keep stopping to adjust them, wasting a lot of time. Always test your props in the same way they'll be used in the shoot. That's the takeaway here. On a tight schedule, nothing can go wrong. It will really ding you.

When you have nine days to do a feature, the actors get one, maybe two takes. There simply is no time to do take after take, hoping you'll get the perfect performance. This is why casting great actors is still important in a lower-budget movie. They have to get it right, right away. This means you have to direct differently. If you need a glance from an actor to cut the scene, shoot the glance because there's no time to run the entire scene for it again. You have to shoot only what you need. Your actors have to be cool and able to jump all over the place to get the scene shot quickly and efficiently. If you have a star with an ego, this style can be an issue. Many star actors with some ego would prefer you let them go through the entire scene without interrupting them, and to do otherwise would somehow be rude.

Every second counts on a lower budget or tightly scheduled movie. If a lightbulb goes out, and it takes ten minutes to replace it, those minutes add up. Props, wardrobe, everything needs to be ready to go as soon as they are needed. No moment can be wasted.

Being able to direct a feature-length movie in nine or ten days is fucking hard. I've done it. It is much harder than shooting a movie in a month. But that's what I was working with, and I was getting the movies done. For what little money we had, they were pretty damn good—at least good enough to get me brought back to the party.

Directing on a spaceship set for Atlantic Rim 2.

Alien Predator (2018)

I had been doing movie after movie, most of them shot on a Red cinema camera. So I thought, "Why not get one of my own?" I figured I could rent the camera to any production I joined, and when I wasn't working, I could rent it out to other productions. It turned out to be a great investment.

When I got my Red Dragon secondhand from a retiring DP, I went around Los Angeles and shot all sorts of test footage. I was obsessed. I was finally able to get studio-quality images by myself. It's one thing to shoot on a Red camera and another to own one. My Black Magic pocket camera was awesome, but this camera would be able to shoot the movies I worked on.

I decided that whatever movie I directed next, I was also going to shoot it myself.

I don't consider myself a cinematographer, but in the spirit of pushing myself, I wanted to try. I even forked over a stack of cash and took the prestigious ASC Master Class to learn from two of the best cinematographers in the world, Dante Spinotti and Newton Thomas Sigel. Watching them light a scene was like watching the conductor of a world-class symphony. It was beautiful.

When my phone rang, it was David Latt, a partner at The Asylum. He was wondering if I would be available to direct a nine-day mockbuster of Shane Black's *The Predator* titled *Alien Predator*. I said, "Let's rock."

While I was definitely not a world-class cinematographer, I showed The Asylum some footage I shot on my Red. They reviewed my work and approved me as the cinematographer, and I was off to the races.

Preproduction for *Alien Predator* was different from the preproduction on all the other movies I'd done before. Before, I would usually be buried in the script, but now I had my Red Dragon and Xeen lenses in my living room. I was shooting all sorts of lens tests and building out my handheld and easy rig. I wanted to shoot the entire movie handheld, which I did.

The script was a straightforward story about a group of soldiers who bump into killer aliens. Although I was directing, I was more concerned with the cinematography than anything else. I mitigated my anxiety by hiring a great gaffer and DP, Nathaniel Elegino, and my B cam operator was Josh Maas, who had shot for me many times. With what amounted to two other DP's, our footage looked Netflix-quality good.

Since we shot entirely handheld, I got a workout every day as I lugged around my camera rig. It never felt that heavy when I started the day, but by the end, it weighed a ton. I walked away sore and with a newfound respect for camera operators.

This time, because I was actually operating the camera, I got compositions that I normally wouldn't have called for. Holding the camera with your body connects you to the frame differently.

While I became a better cinematographer and camera operator by focusing on cinematography, I think my directing might have suffered. It was a two-camera shoot, meaning I only saw what the other camera shot during playback. Since we were on a tight schedule, I didn't always have time to check, and you don't know what you don't see.

My camera operating may have been solid, and I'm glad I stepped outside my comfort zone, but I don't intend to do that again anytime soon. I might grab the camera for a shot or two, but I'm just fine having a DP and camera operator do the heavy lifting so I can focus on the big picture.

We wrapped the shoot, and once I showered off all the sweat and grime, I looked in the mirror at my new bulging biceps and all the veins protruding in my forearms. When the soreness dissipated and the editor and I had put together a solid cut, I was delighted to have the producers compliment the cinematography. Whatever else they might have said about the movie didn't matter. I was just happy they didn't hate my cinematography.

Shooting and directing Alien Predator.

TV Movie Madness

After *Alien Predator*, I was again back to the grind. Anyone who works freelance knows the feeling. You need to find more work, and my next work was some TV movies.

There is an art to the TV movie, a look that most go for. It's high-key lighting, safe, not too dark, and everyone looks beautiful. The TV movie world has all sorts of rules about sex and violence, what is or isn't acceptable, and they're constantly changing. For the most part, you don't want to be too violent, too scary, or show too much skin, or you run the risk of the network not picking it up. With all these rules, following a formula is your best bet.

I had directed quite a few Lifetime thrillers, and it was time for quite a few more. I still hadn't given up on my action script, *Reactor*, and held on to my dreams of bigger and better movies, but this was my reality. I couldn't complain and risk sounding ungrateful. In the end, I really was grateful that I could keep making movies.

I went on to shoot *A Mother's Greatest Fear* back-to-back with *Stressed to Death*, both of which I was instructed to keep to the formula. When you agree to shoot a movie formulaically, you become more of a craftsman than an artist. I accepted the mission and set out to make the best made-for-TV movie I could with what I had. The aesthetics were safe, I kept the camera on a dolly or slider, shot hardly any handheld, and the actors were all beautifully lit. The cinematographers did their job perfectly.

To keep myself stimulated on *Stressed to Death*, I switched gears and put my full attention toward working with the actors. I had always worked with the actors to some extent, but I decided to really dive in with them on this. I wanted to push the actors and see how far I could take it. David Fincher and Stanley Kubrick are famous for making their actors do a hundred takes and using psychological tactics to get actors to cry. I thought I'd try that out a bit.

I invoked emotion, real fear, and tears by experimenting with methods to push the actors to drum up past events or real people in their lives. I explained to our lead, Gina Holden, that it really was her child who was kidnapped and perhaps dead—that she really was the mother trying to save her.

We did take after take as I demanded more emotion each time, calling for more visible fear. For the most part, the actors embraced my hands-on approach. It felt like I was really in there with them, and I believe they appreciated it. Most were open to this style of direction, but I received pushback from an actor who told me to just let them act. In that case, I let up and let them do their thing. If an actor isn't going to play ball with method directing, I don't want to get tyrannical and insist. Forcing someone to think of a loved one in danger or to imagine their child is kidnapped can be traumatizing. You ultimately want to have a good relationship with your cast, so pissing them off usually isn't a good thing. If you do employ intense character work with your actors, I suggest you discuss your intentions and style of working before hiring them to make sure there's no conflict.

We didn't do many camera setups on that set and instead I got more takes than I usually would. Something happens when you say, "Go again," after take four. The mood shifts slightly. It's almost like the performers are asking why you're going again. And everyone on the set can feel it. I wanted to try different things, and I even gave the actors different direction for some takes so we would have an alternate version of the scene to cut different ways.

This style of directing sure got a lot of emotion. I revved up the drama every chance I could, twisting it in new, different ways. Without being able to express my artistic side with camera moves, I pushed the actors to deliver. Their performances were explosive, raw, and volatile. It was different from anything I'd done before, and I wondered if I had been directing wrong the whole time. Maybe method directing was the better approach.

While I engaged with the cast differently and tried some new techniques, when I watched the movie edited together, I felt as if I overdirected some moments. Some of the subtleties disappeared into drama that felt too big or called attention to itself when it didn't need to. One scene involved our main antagonist plotting her revenge for the death of her husband, and I pushed the performance to be bigger, more volatile. In hindsight, I think the scene would've worked better if it was played or directed smaller. Not every dramatic scene needs tears to be excellent. It's great to want to explore and try new tricks as a filmmaker, but you should understand there's no changing what you did yesterday. Unless you have money to burn, whatever you shoot is what you've got.

Letting the scene find itself and develop organically is an art that I've come to pursue. How a director responds to the actors is the real measure of greatness. You must be collaborative enough to listen and firm enough to commit. If you feel there should be more intensity in a scene, call for it, but don't overdo the moment. Film is about subtlety. Sometimes the actors you think are awesome on set are actually overacting, and the actors you think aren't doing enough are way better when it's all cut together.

Stressed to Death came together well and aired on TV, but like other movies, it went into the ether. No critic wrote about how the acting in this movie was so much better than others I'd done. In fact, I don't think the critics wrote much of anything.

I had done a bunch of TV movies, so I was really hankering to do something a little more meaningful. No insult to TV movies—they certainly have a lucrative place in the market—but the artist in me was craving more. Sometimes things in life work out, sometimes they don't, and sometimes both things can happen at the same time. Other times, life can also get insane, and that's what happened next.

Behind the scenes of Stressed to Death with DP Patrice Lucien Cochet, Gaffer Nathaniel Elegino, and key grip Alex Niknejad.

The Lynyrd Skynyrd Chapter

It all started with a conversation with my good friend Brian Perera. Brian had one of the original band members of Lynyrd Skynyrd, Artimus Pyle, signed to his record label, Cleopatra Records. Brian and Artimus had discussed a movie about the famous Lynyrd Skynyrd plane crash, and Brian asked me if I was interested in directing.

Initially I was overwhelmed by the responsibility of such an endeavor. I'd never made a movie about a real-life incident, and this was a well-known event in rock-and-roll history. I processed my options: If I screwed this up, I would be done for sure. However, if I made a good movie, it could be something great. Something I could hang my hat on. Whatever homework needed to be done, I was ready for it to become my obsession. I was in.

For the next few months, I pored over every Lynyrd Skynrd lyric, book, video, and article—anything I could get my hands on. Artimus flew in and met with me for days of interviews, and I asked him a million questions. His story is a crazy one: the man survived a plane crash, saved people's lives, and then got shot while trying to help. He told the story with tears in his eyes, recounting how he lost his best friend, Ronnie Van Zant. It was hard to not get emotional listening to him. I made sure to take as many notes as possible, and I even filmed our conversation so I could go back.

I had no outline for the script, but I needed to be well informed before I began. Studying eased my anxiety about the project, and I devoured so much Lynyrd Skynyrd content that I would end up already knowing stories before reading another person's account of them. Thankfully, Artimus connected me with Dean Goodman, a respected British journalist and author who wrote a comprehensive book about Artimus's life. Dean and I spent time at his house in the Hollywood Hills, going over the script and debating the facts. I knew I was knowledgeable when I was able to have in-depth conversations with Dean because that man knows everything. His help was tremendous.

The script was, of course, told through the eyes of Artimus Pyle, but I needed his world in my head to write it. I hadn't even been born when the plane crashed in 1977, so not only did I study the music, I studied the era. I watched films from the sixties like *Cool Hand Luke* and *The Flight of the Phoenix* for inspiration. I also referenced movies from the seventies, like *The Buddy Holly Story*, and watched every aeronautical disaster movie I could. After watching *Flight, Sully*, and ten other movies about plane crashes, I almost had a panic attack flying home to visit my family.

When I finally wrote "The End," I couldn't believe it. I felt like I needed to do more research and verify more facts. There was no way I was going to send out the script. I spent another few weeks mulling over every word and scene until my head was about to pop. The dialogue had to be period correct, so there couldn't be any slang that hadn't been used yet. I knew this film would be under a microscope, so I made sure everything was bulletproof. I would call Artimus and ask him if people said things like "cool" or "groovy," and he would correct me if I was off the mark.

Trembling with anxiety, I composed an email and attached the script. I was so fucking nervous. I poured a shot of whiskey, slammed it down, and clicked send. There was no going back now.

With a script ready, we still needed everything else. My housemate, John Mehrer, came on to line produce, and he hired top-level folks. Our fantastic costume designer, Lisa Norcia, had done hit movies like *Whiplash* and *The Purge*, and our production designer had worked on *American Horror Story*. This was not my usual crew; these were union people with big credits.

John rented out a big production office in Hollywood for us to prep. With these high-level people around, it was feeling like a big-budget show, and because it was a Lynyrd Skynyrd movie, people's attitudes were a little more serious.

One difference between low-budget and big-budget prep is the director's itinerary. Every day for a month, I had meetings lined up, broken down, and scheduled well in advance. Both John and I were pushing to make the movie the best it could be, but wanting the best of everything meant the budget was going up.

Luckily our producer, Brian, saw the movie's potential and continued to finance our overages. No producer wants to spend more than was originally allotted, but Brian wanted the movie to turn out well and I was grateful.

As we prepped the shoot, news articles about the movie started popping up in *Rolling Stone, Deadline,* and *The Hollywood Reporter.* Artimus was on the radio, podcasts, and TV, telling the world about the movie. It was exciting that he was drawing a lot of attention to our production, and word about us was spreading around town. But eyeballs on your movie can have consequences, but I'm getting ahead of myself.

I knew the cast of this movie was super important. Brian didn't want stars. He wanted fresh faces, so we set out to find unknown actors to portray the band members. They needed to not only be able to act but also resemble the people they played—and ideally, they'd know how to play the associated musical instrument. That is a tall order, but I was confident if we went through enough headshots, we'd find a good bunch. This is Los Angeles, I kept saying. We would totally get lucky.

Our casting director, Shelby Holt, held session after casting session and looked through literally thousands of submissions for each role.

We saw actors that looked the part but couldn't act it, and actors who could act the part but didn't look right. Casting people who have to look like other people and also play a particular musical instrument is like finding half a needle in a double haystack.

However, I was right about one thing: this is LA. After enough casting sessions and many rounds of auditions and callbacks, we managed to find seven actors to portray the original members of Lynyrd Skynyrd. Because we held so many auditions, not only did we find actors who could look and act the parts, most of them even had the musical skills needed. These actors were cool young guys who were excited to be in the movie. They all hung out with each other and bonded while we sent them off to practice playing Skynyrd songs. When Artimus flew in to meet and jam with them, they heard the story from his mouth, and it made things that much more real for everyone.

We rented a working airplane for some shots and pieces of a broken plane for others. We then had the broken parts craned into the woods to resemble the actual crash site. I insisted on the crash site being an exact replica. People died there, so we had to do it justice out of respect.

I was nervous before day one. In fact, my nerves were so high I was having trouble sleeping a few days out. This was by far the biggest-budget movie I had done, and it was also about one of the most famous bands ever. However, I was determined to not be an insomniac like I was on *Hold Your Breath.*

With sleeping pills and a glass of red wine, I got the rest I needed, and the coffee and Red Bull took care of the grogginess in the morning. I was as good as I was going to be. I stormed the set and took charge. My directing was decisive, and I had high expectations for our rock-star crew. As expected, everyone delivered. The clothes, the sets—they were all so authentic I was loving what I was seeing. The cast was killing it on screen; they acted like a real band, and it all felt right.

The set had a giant thirty-foot crane, bigger than any I'd ever used. Those crane shots came out gorgeous. We had hundreds of extras, and we shot on two Arri Alexa minis with Cooke anamorphic lenses. Everything was the best of the best. The budget had skyrocketed, and I was feeling pressure from Brian, but I was also really excited because everything looked amazing. When things are going well, that usually means something really fucked up is going to happen.

On day eight, with over a hundred extras on set, the union showed up. By union, I mean the International Alliance of Theatrical and Stage Employees. They had come to organize our nonunion show, which I had only heard of happening to other people but not experienced myself. Six union representatives showed up and handed ballots out for the crew to vote on whether or not they wanted the production to become a union show. The vote went in favor of the union, and suddenly they refused to return to work unless the producers came to set and signed the new union contract.

I could do nothing but anxiously pace back and forth and watch the time go by.

Brian and his lawyer had to handle the matter because only a producer could sign the contract. It's LA, so no matter where you are, there's always a shit ton of traffic. By the time Brian arrived, lunch was well over, and we were losing valuable shooting time.

I was upset—all I wanted to do was to get back to making the movie. Every filmmaker knows that time is all you have to make your movie, and only money can buy you more time. But the budget was already maxed out. Any time we lost would not be recovered, ever.

Brian had no choice but to sign their contract, after which the union representatives gave a speech that the entire crew applauded. Neither Brian nor his attorney clapped.

We lost about three hours of filming that day, which was supposed to be the biggest day of the shoot. This was my only chance to make the opening scene work, and I'd been working on it for over a year at that point. There were ten camera setups I wanted to get, and I was only able to shoot two of them. I was so pissed off, and my mood remained soured for most of the shoot.

Despite the unexpected interruption, I was still making the movie I wanted to make, and I was happy with how it was turning out. The DP, Pascal, was shooting beautiful images, and the actors were bringing it. Don't get me wrong, I was stressed, but I was doing my best to keep it together and keep moving.

If the union showing up wasn't enough drama, lawyers from the Lynyrd Skynyrd estate sent out cease-and-desist letters that arrived the very next day. According to the estate, Artimus had signed a consent decree in the eighties that prevented him from being involved in a movie about the band, or so they said. It spooked me since I was named on some of the legal documents. I wasn't sure if someone would show up and shut us down once they filed an injunction to stop all filming.

Regardless, I kept on making the movie while tuning out the cease-and-desist letters. I had no plans to cease or desist. I was angry that someone was trying to shut us down, and that anger reinvigorated me.

Making matters worse, a few days later some of the actors followed the union's suit and refused to work until they were provided more compensation. I was so baffled I thought it was a joke at first.

I had never heard of actors doing this before and have not seen it since. When I told Brian what was going on, again burning valuable shooting time, Brian handled it. The actors got a few extra bucks, and we all went back to shooting the movie, but that incident had made the bad taste in my mouth even worse. Don't get me wrong, there were some really awesome people on the set, but all that shit plus cease-and-desist letters was a bit overwhelming.

After wrapping, I slept for a good two days straight. The editor and I then worked tirelessly to polish the cut as best we could.

However, before we picture locked—that is, finished the edit—we got sued. The movie was officially locked up by a federal court in New York. All work on the film came to a grinding halt because there was no point in spending more to finish if the film would never come out.

Since I was the writer and director, my emails and text messages to Artimus became legal evidence. I had to fly to New York to give a deposition. Let me tell you, sitting at a conference table while getting grilled by a team of high-priced lawyers is not fun, though it's an experience I certainly won't forget.

They were trying to make the case that Artimus was not allowed to tell his life story. The documents they kept referencing were long and filled with legalese, but I became obsessed. I listened to the oral arguments numerous times, and I thought we had a real fighting chance at winning the case. I was anxious as fuck, waiting months and months without knowing when we would get a decision. I was afraid the movie would be banned forever, and that fucked me up. I was too stressed to even leave my apartment some days. I would just drink and check the government site for an update, clicking refresh every five minutes. Then my phone rang.

We lost the case.

The judge ruled in favor of the estate, and the movie was to be permanently banned and all footage deleted. I am not a wall-punching type of guy, but I slapped the shit out of a water bottle that day. I'm not sure if the feelings I experienced were suicidal or homicidal, but I knew I wanted to die and take everyone out with me.

Years of my work would be deleted. There would be no Lynyrd Skynyrd movie, just memories. In fact, even behind-the-scenes photos had to be deleted, so even the memories would be destroyed.

What hit me next was textbook clinical depression. Losing the lawsuit deteriorated my mental state beyond repair. I had put my heart and soul into the project, and it all came crashing down. This loss, coupled with the stress of trying to succeed in an industry that didn't seem to want me, affected my attitude. I grew bitter—angry at the world and angry at the decisions I'd made.

I pushed everyone around me away. A bad attitude doesn't fare well in a relationship, so it became the demise of my relationship with Sara. Once engaged, I was now an angry, sad mess. Not even I wanted to be around me, so how could I expect anyone else to want to? I was heartbroken. Not only was I depressed—I was alone.

As a single, unemployed man who lost his day in court, I drank and smoked more. I was grumpy, heartbroken, and hated life. I felt like a total fucking loser. If a Lynyrd Skynyrd song came on the radio, which happened quite a lot, I couldn't bear to hear it. I had to turn it off or escape. It was too painful.

I was never going to get out of the low-budget movie world. Hell, maybe I would never make another movie again. But I wasn't the only one going through it; so was Brian. They froze all his bank accounts for a period of time, and he was stressed as fuck. With everything going on at the time, we put down a lot of Jack Daniels.

Then, a few weeks later, a glimmer of hope came from the attorneys. We weren't going away so easily. It was time to fight back. I didn't know much about how federal courts work, but I was about to find out. We appealed to the second circuit with three new judges who had the power to overturn the decision to block the movie. This was the last chance I had of having any kind of real career in Hollywood. This was also the last chance this movie had of ever coming out. The lawyers went to war again, and I was watching every step of the way.

Every step of the legal process takes time, and the waiting hurts. Then, one day, the waiting was interrupted. Out of seemingly nowhere, almost every major studio in America including Universal, HBO, NBC, Warner Brothers, Fox, Paramount, and

MGM, among others, wrote amicus briefs on our behalf. They said that if the court upheld its decision, then the First Amendment right to make biopics would be negatively affected. Thirteen other major press organizations and First Amendment rights groups joined in and wrote on our behalf. All of a sudden, this case was important to the future of biopics and freedom of speech everywhere. It was amazing. The studios were paying attention to our film. Major publicity followed, and my name and the name of the movie popped up in *Rolling Stone*, the *New York Times*, and plenty of other publications. It felt good to get publicity, but I was still nervous we weren't going to win the appeal. Would a federal court in New York give a shit about what Hollywood studios had to say? Nobody knew anything.

The anxiety was crippling. All I could think about was the verdict. I would log on to the court's website and check for updates constantly. Sometimes I'd be sitting in front of my computer, just clicking the refresh button. There would be no forewarning when a decision came. It would just come. And it did not come by refreshing my browser. It came in a call from Brian one early morning.

We'd won the appeal.

The court's decision was overturned, and the movie was now allowed to come out. It was arguably the greatest day of my life. Instead of chugging whiskey, I popped champagne. I cried tears of joy as I blasted "Free Bird" in my Sherman Oaks apartment.

It was an emotional rollercoaster where the pain-to-pleasure ratio was poorly skewed. If I had felt as much pleasure from winning as I did pain from losing, I'd be a very happy guy for a long time.

Regardless, I was elated for the time being. I had literal dreams of finishing this movie and nightmares that it would never come out.

We put amazing music and visual effects in it, and *Street Survivors: The True Story of the Lynyrd Skynyrd Plane Crash* turned out incredibly well. It wasn't the big, career-changing hit I hoped it would be, but it got accepted to a few film festivals and is still doing well today. I consider it one of my best movies. The actors were fantastic, it felt authentic to the period, the tone felt real, and it went on to win Best Picture and Best Cinematography at the Hollywood Reel Independent film festival.

Artimus loved the movie, and at the end of the day, I was so glad he could tell the story of what really happened that day.

The union incident and all the other behind-the-scenes drama can be seen on a full-length making-of documentary, directed by our stealthy EPK shooter, the talented Jeff Leroy. Check it out at https://jaredcohn.com/movies/. You can see me directing and looking like a crazy man. I was so impassioned, I come across as a lunatic.

Directing Street Survivors: The True Story of the Lynyrd Skynyrd Plane Crash.

The world premiere of Street Survivors, at the Hollywood Reel Independent Film Festival.

Devil's Revenge (2018)

During the lengthy legal war with Lynyrd Skynyrd, I directed a music video for Brian for the song "Rudolph the Red-Nosed Reindeer" performed by William Shatner and ZZ Top's Billy Gibbons. It was a rock-and-roll party scene, complete with confetti, hula hoopers, and breakdancers.

As a *Star Trek* fan, having the opportunity to direct William Shatner in a music video was pretty cool. At this point, I had worked with a lot of familiar faces, so the days of geeking out were over, but when you meet someone you watched as a kid, a little part of you smiles.

After the shoot, Shatner, Brian, and I got to talking about movies. Apparently, years before, Shatner had developed a screenplay with Maurice Hurley, one of the original *Star Trek* writers. The script sounded pretty cool: it was about an archaeologist and called *La Reliquia*. Brian was interested in producing a Shatner movie, and I was interested in directing a Shatner movie.

Working with Shatner on a music video was great, but to do an actual movie with a multimillion-dollar budget with him would be incredible. The script was a fascinating blend of science fiction with horror and action elements. Originally Shatner was going to play the hero, but now he would be playing the hero's adventurous father.

Before he agreed to let me direct, Shatner wanted to hear my vision. I figured I had better do a thorough breakdown of the script to really articulate how I would go about bringing this screenplay to life. If I didn't, he would think I wasn't worthy.

The script called for contained underground labyrinths and demonic altars where researchers would search for an ancient artifact. I figured the best place to build these sets would be inside a cave. I had looked around locally, but there are barely any caves in California. I would have to do some more digging.

I searched for the most interesting caves in America and discovered Kentucky is full of them, ones with giant stalagmites and even underwater megacaves. I put together a visual presentation and explained my plan for shooting it with anamorphic lenses and a practical demon suit made by a top creature maker. The presentation contained some images of the Predator suit and other scary images as inspiration for our monsters. Brian and I set up a meeting in Shatner's office on Ventura Boulevard, and I gave it my best shot, showing off the locations I found and what I thought the demons should look like.

Shatner approved of Kentucky and was in fact very familiar with the area, as he owned a home there. We discussed the architecture in Louisville and a potential cast for the movie, and just like that, we were shaking hands. I was Shatner approved.

Given that the late, great screenwriter Maurice Hurley wrote for the original *Star Trek*, which Shatner had starred in, we considered building our cast from within the *Star Trek* community. I grew up watching Jeri Ryan who played Seven of Nine, a former drone of one of the most menacing bad guys in *Star Trek: The Next Generation*, the Borg. I knew it would be a long shot to get her, but I still wanted to try.

Since Jeri was a big star, she was expensive. I told Brian I would love to have her and that having her would make the film more valuable, which is true. The more big names you have in your movie, the more your movie will sell for. Luckily, Brian does things big, so he pulled the trigger and agreed to her fee. I hugged Brian, stoked to have such a killer cast. The next thing I knew, I was flying from LA to Louisville, Kentucky.

With six weeks to prep, I spent my days meeting with the crew, casting, and location scouting. In the evenings, I'd roam around Louisville, admiring the distinguished architecture and drinking all sorts of delicious whiskeys. The Skynyrd trial was still going on, so I was stressed out about that, but I was also happy to be working and keeping my mind occupied. The opportunity to work with Shatner was incredible, and I didn't want to blow it by stressing about another movie. I did my best to compartmentalize and keep myself focused on the present.

The first day I rolled to set, half the city of Louisville was there asking for Shatner. I had no idea how people found out where we would be—word must spread quickly in a small town. Naively, I told one excited reporter that I was the director and happy to give an interview, but the reporter was not interested. They wanted Shatner. Unfortunately for them, he wasn't even there that day.

After we shot some scenes in the city, it was time to go to the caves. Caves can be tricky to film in because some are privately owned while others are owned by the city, and all of them have their own rules about what you can and cannot do inside them.

Despite bringing in lights, generators, and rigging equipment, we couldn't attach anything to the walls of the caves, and some sections were off-limits entirely. In some caves, you couldn't even touch the walls. I had no idea there were so many rules, but caves were more sensitive than I'd thought.

We had one spectacular cave just outside of Louisville pretty much locked down. We were just waiting on the final signature for permission. The scene called for a steep slope inside a cave, and we had been all over town looking for the perfect spot, only to find it there. We spoke with the town and then with one official and then another. Nobody seemed to know who the ultimate authority was on whether or not we could film in this one particular cave. Time was running out, and a couple of days before we were going to shoot, we were told we wouldn't be allowed to film there at all. It was a bummer. We had major stars, and if we had a shitty location, it would not be a good day.

We needed a backup cave with a steep slope, and we needed it fast. It was a scramble to check out alternative locations with some sort of a slope. Stopping at one, I rushed inside the darkness without thinking. With my iPhone flashlight on, I looked around for a workable slope. When I took a step forward, my leg disappeared through a hole in the ground, sending my phone flying from my hand. Landing on my face, I was left in pitch blackness. I breathed heavily for a moment, the sounds of my every movement echoing off the walls. After a struggle, I managed to pull myself out of the hole and find my phone in the darkness. I pointed the light toward where my leg had fallen through, and underneath the hole was a thirty-foot drop to deadly spikes below. If I had taken one step further, I could have fallen to my death. I was more careful moving forward and stopped rushing into strange places. We wouldn't shoot any scenes there and found our slope somewhere else.

The production shot all over Louisville and at many caves. At the time, it felt awesome just to be working on a movie that was definitely coming out, unlike the Skynyrd movie which was still held up in court. I had high hopes for *La Reliquia*, which was later called *Devil's Revenge*. While it did well and got good reviews, it was still a low-budget genre-horror movie. It was not Sundance material. WME did not call me, nor did any agent, and it felt like I was right back where I'd started.

Lighting fires on location in Kentucky for Devil's Revenge.

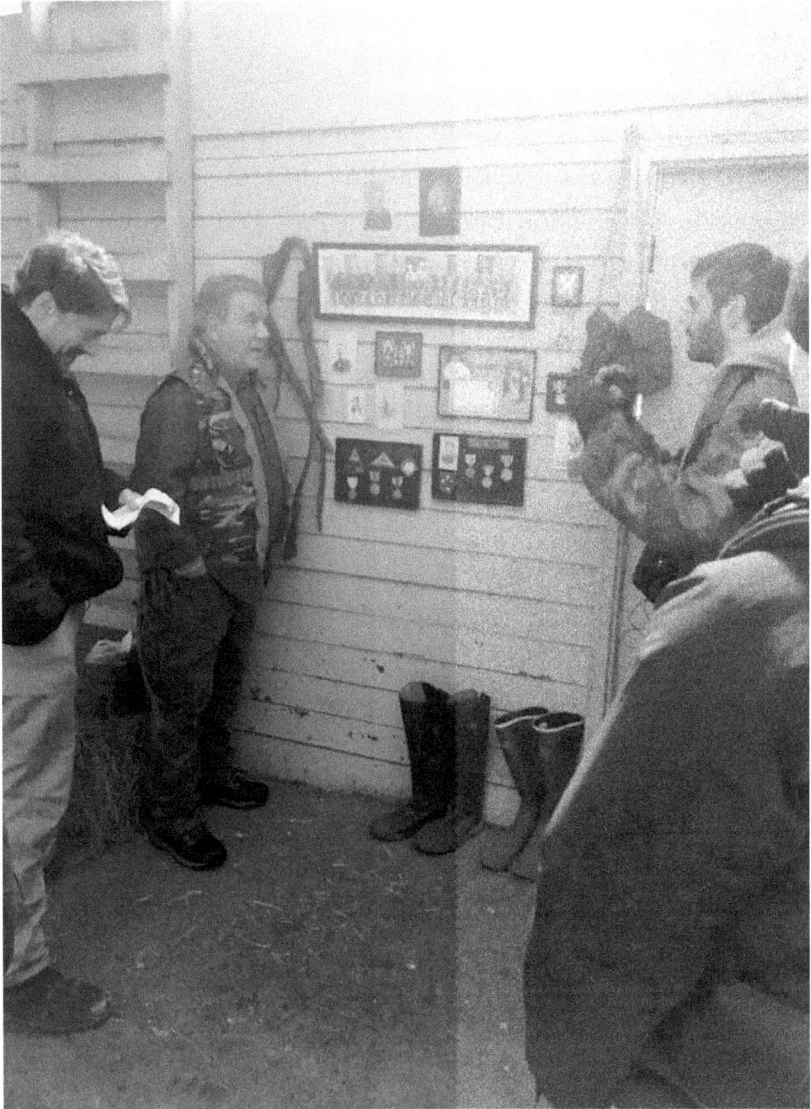

Directing William Shatner and Jason Brooks in Devil's Revenge, in Kentucky.

Powering Through

I would continue to write, but the only calls I was getting were for more low-budget movies. It was time to look in the mirror and accept reality: I was a low-budget movie guy. That was okay for now. I felt grateful to be working, and that helped me feel better about my situation, and the future looked a bit brighter.

I either realized or justified to myself that being artistically satisfied isn't about the size of the budget. It's about the quality of the art being created. Filmmaking is an art form, and I swore whatever film I did next would be worthy of being called art.

However, that art flick would be a Lifetime thriller called *American Psychos*, originally titled *Psycho BFF*. This time I threw out the formulaic playbook. I decided to scratch my artistic itch and do as many scenes as possible in a single shot. It didn't matter if this was a Lifetime movie: the artist in me insisted I approach this film differently.

The camera team was warned it was going to be a challenging project because of how I wanted to shoot. Luckily, we had a fantastic gimbal operator, David Minadeo, who had a Ronin 2 with a Ready Rig and strong arms to keep the long shots going.

I had never shot a movie with this many long and elaborate camera moves before. Choreographing a moving camera with moving actors while still telling a story feels like a ballet. It's higher level, more thoughtful filmmaking.

We were tracking actors for minutes-long shots. However, after trying and failing a five-minute shot a few times, you begin to wonder if you will ever get a good take. We'd peppered the ground with actor and camera marks to be precise, but getting basic coverage or playing it safe would have been much easier. Using time as a negating factor feels unartistic, but that's reality. When it starts raining on take fifteen, you want to give up on the shot, but you shouldn't. I didn't, and come take twenty-three, we nailed it.

For example, in the opening scene, we shot two girls walking on a bridge, and one girl shoves the other off. The camera follows the body as it goes over the edge and reveals the dead girl at the bottom. To pull off this complex shot, we tracked backward on a gimbal as the two girls walked and argued. When they stopped mid-bridge, the camera pushed into the evil girl's face while we swapped the other girl out with a crash dummy. As the camera pulled back, it caught and followed the tail end of the dummy going over the bridge. On the ground, the dummy was swapped with a human body double so when the camera panned over the ledge, there was a real body.

There were a lot of moving parts, and we needed a lot of hands to make them work, but it was worth it.

Since I had shot the movie mostly in oners, editing was bound to be easy, so I decided to take it on by myself. I spent a few weeks back in front of my computer with Adobe Premiere. At first, it was nostalgic since I hadn't edited a feature in years. I liked it for a few days and then I hated it.

It's not that editing is hard. It's when the computer crashes or lags that's a bitch. That and the exporting and rendering; all the waiting makes that tedious work more painful. I had burned my brain out editing for so many years, and it all came flooding right back. After the first cut was finished, I handed the project off to another editor. It's not that I couldn't finish it, but it needed to get done, and I'd had enough of a refresher on why I stopped editing. I am happy to have the skill, but I am equally happy to not be an editor.

The movie aired, and I was certain at least one or two review sites would mention the complex camera work we did. Nope. The general audience and even critics did not give a single fuck.

Our strong gimbal operator, David Minadeo.

On to the Next Thing

***

Although I was doing a lot of made-for-TV movies, I hadn't actually done any straight-up TV. Many people who make movies want to make TV and vice versa, so I jumped at the chance to spend six weeks in Georgia directing three episodes of *The Encounter*, a popular series on a faith-based channel called Pureflix.

When I checked out the show, it seemed well done but shot in a pretty basic way. I was given three scripts to read for the episodes I was about to direct, and since this show was a faith-based drama, they all had a lot of dialogue and not much action. However, one episode called "Crosshairs" stood out. It was set in the Gulf War and involved a rescue mission. Between the lines of a dramatic heart-to-heart were moments of action that called for some military combat. In this, I saw an opportunity to give the episode epic battle scenes.

The Encounter producers were initially taken aback by my plan, but I was insistent. I had been hired to direct, and this was what I wanted to do. If possible, I was determined to make it a miniversion of *Apocalypse Now*, complete with gun battles, snipers, and mortar explosions going off everywhere.

Adding combat action into what was really a drama felt a little bit like sneaking in something that wasn't supposed to be there. But when the producers and the writer himself saw what I was doing, they liked it and let me continue.

We turned fireworks upside down to sell them as mortar explosions and had actors run through billowing smoke while dodging bullets.

The crew even used paintball guns filled with dust pellets that simulated an authentic gunshot.

All the extra combat was me putting my stamp on the project. I could've simply shot what was on the page, but I saw an opportunity to go bigger and give more spectacle. I was learning how to push better, or rather how to justify getting what I wanted with valid arguments. Doing the episode my way made it way more interesting to me, and to my delight, producers liked it as well.

After six weeks in Georgia, the time to return to LA had come. It's always a bit bittersweet leaving a project on location. You connect with a lot of good people and make friends. It's like a little family, and then it's all over. Production would go on to film another six episodes with three different directors, but I was on an airplane flying back home, unemployed once again.

Directing in Georgia the episode "Crosshairs" for the series The Encounter.

Shark Season (2020)

I thought wearing masks in LA would last a week or two. At first it was fun to Zoom with friends and play board games, but after a couple of weeks of not being able to leave home due to COVID, I went fucking stir-crazy.

COVID affected the entire industry. A lot of big studios stopped creating, and productions shut down. Good people lost work. However, with the lack of new content being made, a window opened for producers who were brave enough to create during uncertain times.

I felt bad about people dying, of course, but I was not cut out to sit at home. Something needed to change, anything, so when David Latt called asking if I wanted to go to Florida for a shark movie, I said, "Hell, yes!" What better way to escape COVID purgatory than to make a movie in Florida, where there was no such thing as a lockdown? In fact, all the restaurants, bars, and clubs were still very much in business. I dove in full force, grateful to be busy and distracted from ordinary life. Moviemaking is way more exciting than sitting around playing checkers online.

We had done some casting in LA and crewed up, which was more difficult than normal. Not many people wanted to go to Florida to do a movie when almost every other state was enforcing a lockdown. I can't say I blame them. We were in a global pandemic that was unlike anything we'd ever seen before.

After assembling a fearless team of filmmakers, we prepared to travel to Florida for the sake of making a movie in turbulent times. I am grateful for everyone who took the job because it sure was a crazy one.

Nobody in Florida was wearing a mask. In fact, if you put one on people would look at you like you were weird. So I took the mask off. When in Rome and all that. Thank God, because I could finally breathe again.

We were working with a local, Roy, to help secure locations: beautiful beaches and areas that we would have full control to shoot at. We were grateful for the help as we didn't know the area well at all. Roy was our local contact for everything. He helped us with permits, locations, traffic control—whatever we needed.

On day one, we were supposed to meet up with Roy on a beautiful beach area for our first shot. The parking lot was quite far from the sand, so without thinking, we decided to drive the equipment onto the beach where the set was. It was hot, and I didn't want our small crew to have to lug over all the gear.

I had seen cars drive on beaches before, and we had a filming permit, so I assumed it would be no problem. Well, it was. Apparently, driving on the beach is a big no-no there, and the police showed up to swiftly kick us out. Afterward Roy congratulated us on being the first film to ever get banned from shooting there in twenty-six years.

Not only did we lose all of our locations on day one, but we were also banned from filming anywhere in the county. Yikes. I'd gotten the production in quite the pickle, and the producers were not happy. They had spent a lot of money to send us to Florida to make a shark movie. I was never one to not deliver when I had a movie to direct, and there was a movie crew and actors with me. I'd be damned if I didn't get it done.

The shoot instantly became a guerrilla project. We had zero permission to film anywhere, which meant we could film anywhere.

Some people were stressed, but I was used to these situations because of my early filmmaking days. If we saw a place we wanted to film, we made sure nobody was around, got the shot, and got out. It was just like I did on *Wishing for a Dream*, except this time I had a crew to keep on the lookout.

We stole locations that we would've never gotten permission to use in the first place. I knew the shots I needed to get, so I kept it efficient. The crew kept a low profile and stealthily moved around town, filming our movie scene by scene. In addition to filming without a permit, I flew my drone around everywhere to get swooping aerial shots. None of it would've been possible with permit regulations.

Coming from a guerrilla-filmmaking background, I found it kind of refreshing to work like this. Filmmaking involves an insane amount of rules and regulations, most of which have good intentions, but more often than not, they just prevent you from doing the things you want.

However, when you break the rules and operate like a gangster, some people can't handle the stress.

One of our main actors, Elle, decided I was a piece-of-shit director that had no clue what I was doing. At this point, I had directed around forty films and worked extremely hard to grow as a filmmaker. To me, Elle was being completely unreasonable. I had tried to reason with her, be nice, and explain why we had to break the rules. But no matter what I said, I wasn't getting through. The situation was what it was: we were guerrilla filmmaking, and she wasn't going with the flow. She told me she didn't trust me and repeatedly threatened to quit.

When she didn't have issues with the shot, she had issues with wardrobe or props. I pulled her aside numerous times to reason with her, but I might as well have been talking to a wall. It was maddening. Every time I blocked a scene, she would tell me I was bad at directing without providing further explanation. I was beyond frustrated.

Of all the movies I've done, I've never butted heads with an actor to the extent I did with Elle. Never before and never since have I wanted an actor gone. I love actors—I was one. I understand it is a hard job, but she was extra special. Maybe she just didn't have it in her to handle the guerrilla lifestyle, and it made everyone else's job ten times harder. I campaigned to have her terminated, but the producers wouldn't budge. I was even having creative discussions with the writer on how to kill her character off and make the movie work with a rewrite. Having an actor treat me like that drove me up a wall, but guerrilla filmmaking is a battle. You must march on. I bit my tongue, put on my baby gloves, walked on eggshells, and did whatever was needed to finish the movie. I wasn't about to lose it over a series of tantrums.

Despite getting banned and the behind-the-scenes drama, we eventually had a movie in the can, and I got myself on an airplane back to Los Angeles.

LA was a ghost town. I was living near Wilshire and La Brea, which are usually busy. But I couldn't see a soul in sight. Not a car on the road or pedestrians on the street. Nothing. And then in the middle of the pandemic, everyone started rioting and burning down the city. LA went from a ghost town to a war zone.

I was back to sitting on my ass like the rest of the city, but I knew I couldn't sit still much longer. I had to take action, or I'd lose my fucking mind. I hadn't stopped in a while, and I had zero intention to start now.

Fearless filmmakers, Joe Tomcufcik, Chris Kaiser, Marcus Friedlander and myself, in Florida, shooting Shark Season during Covid.

Her Deadly Groom (2020)

I had written many spec scripts at this point in my life, and one of them was written years ago during one of many modafinil-fueled writing frenzies. The story was called *Single Mom*, and I thought it would sell as a Lifetime movie. I had already written *Born Bad*, and that did well, so I kind of knew what I was doing.

It was also at this time that my longtime friend and producer Demetrius Stear and his business partner Ace were looking to do a movie. Demetrius was like me. We started as actors and did quite a few independent films but both gravitated toward filmmaking.

Since I had success as a director for hire on Lifetime movies, I sent Demetrius the script for *Single Mom*. Once he read it and we chatted, he decided to move forward and take a chance on the script. *Single Mom* was your classic Lifetime story: a woman meets a charming single guy who turns out to be a bad dude. It was a good script and written to be done cheap, meaning it had few locations and a small cast.

Since we were financing this movie ourselves, we would do whatever we could to save money. Demetrius, Ace, and I lugged C-stands and lights to my SUV and packed it to the brim. We were like an indie rock band, doing all the heavy lifting ourselves.

I was super focused, making sure the shots were lit for Lifetime and that the actors delivered. The art had to look good, the sound needed to be perfect, and every shot had to be 100 percent in focus because the stakes were extraordinarily high. I was feeling the pressure. This movie would have to get acquired by Lifetime for it to be worth it. Demetrius had taken a chance with me on *Death Pool* and *The Domicile*, and we'd lost big. I wasn't going to fuck up again.

We cast the fantastic, Academy-nominated Eric Roberts as the jealous ex-husband. We'd worked together before, and he ad-libbed some gems on that set that I quote to this day. The whole cast delivered, and Nathaniel Elegino, the DP, and I shot one hell of a movie with as many angles as we could capture with our short schedule.

Midway through the shoot, we cut some clips together to show an interested distribution company. They were loving it big time, confident that Lifetime would pick it up. They told us they couldn't wait to see the finished movie. It sounded like we would have a deal, and I was sure we'd be celebrating our success and planning our next movie.

We got through the shoot, and it all worked. Fired up about having a real company interested, we worked painstakingly with the editor to make sure it was as tight as it could possibly be. We spent countless hours going over each shot and frame of the movie, and only when it was good did we send it to the interested distribution company.

We were sure they were going to respond with an offer, but they suddenly decided to pass on the movie without reason. We were baffled. This company was hot on it one second and then just like that, cold as ice. Once again, we were fucked. The majority of my money had been sunk into making this thing, and now it would be another total loss.

I could not believe how bad my track record at producing was. Literally every movie I put my own money into was a loss. To our surprise, the company that passed came back and did us one hell of a solid. Maybe they felt bad for passing, but they were kind enough to connect us with another potential buyer. We sent this new buyer a screener and hoped we would be able to get some of our money back. Well, we got more than some.

The movie sold for more than double what we hoped to get in the first place. Holy shit. It was the biggest win I had ever experienced. For the first time, I had spent my own money on a movie and profited.

We celebrated. We had done the unthinkable: we put a movie together and sold it for good money. It was released as *Her Deadly Groom*, and it was so rewarding to see it come out. I finally felt the burden of life lighten for the first time. For the next twenty-four hours, I was on cloud nine.

Making a movie is actually the easy part. Getting the money together to make the movie is much harder, and getting that money back after making the movie is the hardest part.

But like all joyful moments, our victory was fleeting. The movie came out, got some good reviews, and then faded into the background with the other movies that came out that day. The difference was this time I would be putting money back into my pocket instead of never seeing it again. It opened my eyes and shifted my perspective of what was possible. It's one thing to hear stories about other people's films doing well; it's another when it's your film and you can reap the rewards. I was a director for hire on the vast majority of my films, meaning I didn't have any backend participation. If those films made money, I didn't get an extra cent.

I had glimpsed real financial success, and it felt good. My name was all over the internet, I was doing all sorts of interviews, and this success validated everything else. I finally felt good, and feeling good feels good. But again those feelings are fleeting.

It was time for Demetrius and me to plot our next production.

Academy nominated Eric Roberts, starring in Her Deadly Groom.

Swim (2021)

While Demetrius and I were bouncing ideas around for the next production, I got a call from David Latt, who told me that The Asylum was now in business with Tubi, a hot new advertising video-on-demand platform. Basically, it's free TV and movies but streaming with commercials. Tubi had just been bought by Fox and was blowing up and starting to produce original content. One of their first movies was slated to be *Swim*, a movie about a shark trapped in a house during a storm. David Latt asked me if I was interested in directing. It was an easy yes.

After reading the script, I wondered how the hell would I be able to pull it off. A shark trapped in a house? I recalled the movie *Crawl* about a gator trapped in a house and remembered how awesome that was. I had even gone to a screening of *Crawl* with the French director Alexandre Aja and legendary producer, Sam Raimi. Raimi understands cinema and how audiences will react to things, so to hear him speak about cause and effect was brilliant. The greats are great for a reason. *Crawl* was a masterpiece. I tried to say hi to Raimi and Aja at the end, but so did everyone else, so there were no selfies taken.

That said, the *Crawl* budget was at least $10 million, and *Swim* would have a lot less: half a million dollars and eight days to use it. If the movie came out okay, I was told Fox would push it hard and promote it on their network. I was also told Entertainment Tonight would be covering the shoot. All very glitzy stuff.

I did my homework and studied the behind-the-scenes of *Crawl* to see how they pulled off flooding a house. They had built sets in massive pools, so we were going to build sets in massive pools. As soon as I figured out how to do it, I was all in.

Even though we had a low budget, we had a kick-ass production designer, David Jeter, who perfectly recreated rooms from a house in Malibu, in a backyard pool in the Valley. It was a creative challenge, and I always like challenges because that means I'm pushing myself to do something I haven't done before.

I got a chance to shoot with giant rain towers and multiple water trucks to create a storm, which was fun. It was fascinating to learn all the ins and outs of working with water. One thing we didn't consider was how cold the water from the truck would be. The actors were in bathing suits, so they were quite uncomfortable, especially when we blasted wind at them with giant fans and leaf blowers. It looked great on film, but it didn't feel great. I looked over to the shivering actors about to go back under the rain towers, and for once I was glad not to be one of them.

To make the cast feel better, we had heat packs, heaters, and robes, but those barely helped. They were miserable. During one freezing night in Malibu, one of the actors straight up hyperventilated and had to stop due to being wet and freezing cold. I was concerned, we all were, so we immediately put several space heaters on him and had medics get him going again. Luckily, he was good as soon he warmed up, but he was not a happy camper that evening.

It reminded me of being in Canada for *Feed the Devil*, swimming through a frozen lake. I had been so cold, and we didn't even have heaters, robes, or any of that. It's tough asking a cold actor to take their warm robe off, step away from the heater, and go act like a shark is about to kill them. Still, I needed to complete the movie, so I had to push even when I knew it was hard. Filmmaking is hard. It's asking people to do uncomfortable things, and I had to do that a lot on this show.

The shoot was proving to be more challenging than I expected, and just when I thought enough crazy shit had happened, there was more where that came from. In the middle of lunch one day, halfway into shooting this movie, I heard someone cursing loudly and trashing the set.

A moment later, I see a well-dressed, linebacker-sized dude going postal, storming through the set and ranting that part of his house had been caught in our movie. This hostile neighbor, Bill, marched right through the set, knocking things over and cursing the crew while threatening to beat people up and destroy the equipment. Bill would not leave until he saw all the footage we shot near his house. He seemed paranoid and began talking about his daughter being kidnapped and people wanting him dead. It all sounded a bit much. I was just there to make a movie, and he was getting in the way.

Production kindly informed him that we did not legally have to show him the footage. We had permission to film at the house, and having a neighboring house out of focus is legally allowed on screen. Imagine filming a neighborhood and not being allowed to see the other houses on the block. This dude was off his rocker, but there was no reasoning with him.

Bill then proceeded to scream right in my face and demanded we delete all our footage. As much as I wanted to kick this guy in the nuts, I knew it wasn't the best idea. Calling the cops would just take hours and waste our day. The best thing to do, we decided, was to just show Bill the damn footage and hope his house wasn't seen too much.

We took him to the computer and showed him every clip we shot to prove his house was not in focus. While it could be seen in the distance, it wasn't really visible. Still, Bill huffed and puffed, slammed his fist on the table, and demanded we delete the shots, threatening all kinds of lawsuits if we didn't comply. I was panicking because we'd be in trouble if we deleted those shots, but I also didn't want to be responsible for someone getting sued. Legally we didn't have to delete anything, but if we called the cops, and they came to uber-wealthy Malibu of all places, we'd be dealing with hours of bullshit. It was a nightmare. We simply didn't have time for this.

Our DP and camera wizard, Marcus Friedlander, stepped up to the computer and explained he was going to delete the shots. My heart sank, but I let him work. Marcus dragged the clips into the trash can and emptied it to show the angry neighbor they were really gone. After listening to another painful twenty minutes of paranoid ranting, Bill finally calmed down and left. I asked Marcus if he really deleted the shots. Marcus smirked, opened Red Undead, and recovered the deleted shots. I was relieved and learned that as long as you don't record anything over the deleted shots, there is a way to recover them. Disaster and heart attack averted.

Speaking of heart attacks, the finale of the movie was set to take place at night on the roof, as it was the only way for the characters to escape the shark. Once again, it was freezing. There I was, standing on the roof and barking marching orders with my heavy jacket on. As the scene was set, people kept coming up and up, each carrying more and more heavy equipment. I looked at my feet standing on 1970s residential shingles and wondered if the roof was able to withstand all the weight.

The giant rain towers were being set up, and then the actors would be coming up. More and more gear kept coming until there were forty people on the roof, plus the ton of gear.

I imagined the roof caving in and what a disaster it would be. I almost called off the shot and told everyone to get off the roof. I knew nobody had thought about this—we hadn't discussed the roof's integrity. Then I realized I knew absolutely nothing about how much weight a roof could hold and did my best to not think about it anymore. The roof held no problem. We wrapped the shoot, and thankfully nobody got hurt. Sometimes worries are just that, worries.

On location for Swim, building sets in a swimming pool. Assistant
director, Nathan D. Snyder running the set.

Movie, Movie, Movie

Swim was a fun, campy movie, and I heard it did well on Tubi, so I was feeling good. However, it was time to take the money we made from selling *Her Deadly Groom* and produce another TV movie, *Killer Advice*. After that, it was *Party from Hell* and then yet another one, *A Daughter's Deceit*.

After cranking out a few of these, we were told by a distributor to make a romantic comedy. When a distributor says they want you to make a certain kind of movie, the logical thing to do is make that kind of movie. Never in a million years did I think I would produce a rom-com, but that was what we were doing. We made these movies to make a profit, not to try to win awards at festivals or be artistic. To be honest, I actually enjoy watching romantic comedies. Sometimes it's nice to watch a movie where not everybody dies. With our instructions to make a rom-com, we shot and sold *Love by Design*, a heart-warming story complete with a cute kid and a dog named Mr. Noodles, played by my real dog, Fred.

Demetrius, Ace, and I finally had a working business plan that didn't involve sending cold emails and waiting. Demetrius was and is killing it as a producer, raising money and selling movies, doing everything a good producer should. I'm grateful to have a solid team now capable of dealing with the paperwork, legal deliveries, and all the other things I would hate to do. Also, when you have the money, you have the power to make movies whenever you want. Waiting on people sucks. Needing to be patient sucks. The world does not move on your time, but when you have the money, it tends to respond quicker.

Did I have a problem with my resume being chock-full of made-for-TV Lifetime movies? Was I worried I'd get pigeonholed as a TV movie director? Well, it was better than being the low-budget horror guy; at least now I was a TV guy. Regardless, I could still only play the cards I was dealt. If I wasn't working, I knew that idle hands would do the devil's work. I didn't want that. I was making money, I was busy, I had a career. And in the midst of producing and directing Lifetime movie after Lifetime movie, I was offered yet another Lifetime movie.

Drinking La Croix while directing a TV movie, with producer Demetrius Stear.

Cheer for Your Life (2021)

After flying out of LAX, I was staying in some trailer AirBnb in the middle of Oklahoma with the DP, Josh Maas. I would be there for over a month. Josh and I had been around the world together, and he was always fun to hang out with. We would drink whiskey and smoke spliffs in our downtime, and since we had a month of prep and weren't allowed out of the house due to COVID rules, that meant more whiskey and more weed.

It was a cheerleader movie, which was very popular with the Lifetime crowd for some reason. The plot was strangely dark, following cheerleaders who are forced to have sex with football players in some secret hazing tradition that results in a murder and a mom saving the day. We had a budget of about half a million dollars and fourteen days to make it work, so it seemed easy enough.

I now had the responsibility of casting girls to play the cheerleaders. When I was casting *Bikini Spring Break*, it was fun and exciting to hire pretty girls to be in the movie. I used to joke on set, and the mood was light-hearted. Times had since changed, and people were getting canceled left and right. The #MeToo movement was in full force, so I was scared to even compliment a girl's appearance. I was careful to make sure everything I said couldn't be misinterpreted.

Being a movie director means you've got to be careful. A lot of producers and directors have found themselves canceled. I am not a creep, but even when I think I'm telling a joke, it could be misinterpreted. On more than one occasion, I've said something casually, only to later find out that I made someone cry because they thought I meant something else. Actors can be sensitive, so when you accept the responsibility of being the director, your behavior sets the tone on set.

During wardrobe fittings, when an actress would come to ask if I liked her cheerleading outfit, I would say, "It's acceptable." Some of the actresses replied back with uncertainty, asking if I actually liked it. I felt as though saying "Yeah" might come across as creepy. The next thing I know, I could get canceled because the girl goes on to say, "Jared said he liked the way I looked." Not on my watch. I'd rather be paranoid than in the tabloids.

Once we started the shoot, everything was going swimmingly. We were shooting on a Red Gemini with Cooke lenses, and the pictures were beautiful. The leads, Allison McAtee and Grace Patterson, were delivering fantastic performances, and the locations in Oklahoma were Lifetimey and picturesque. Naturally, that meant something bad had to happen.

We were in some old manor-style house, shooting the climax in the middle of the night. It was the football team against the cheerleaders in the script, and I was in the zone. I marched back and forth between set and video village, Red Bull in one hand, vape in the other. The script was on an iPad mini strapped around my chest, and I had my cap on backward. I was dialed in. The lights were set, the camera was up, and all the actors except one were there. Then someone informed me the missing actor was having a mental breakdown in the bathroom. What?

Of course I hoped she was all right, and there was no point in asking if we could get an ETA for her return. I did the only thing I could do, and that was to shoot everybody else in the scene and then go back the next day to shoot her lines. It wasn't the ideal way to cover a scene, but that was the only solution I had in the moment, and it worked. I got the shot.

With the movie complete, I was excited to see it premiere on the Lifetime Channel instead of the Lifetime Movie Network. There's a big difference.

Then it was back to Los Angeles and reality. Even worse, the holidays were coming up. For years I always dreaded the holidays because it felt like a yearly check-in, and I hadn't gotten where I wanted to be yet. Since Hollywood shuts down at the end of every year, there's nothing you can do but reflect, especially when you're sitting across from your family on Thanksgiving. I was going to go home to New York and do the same holiday thing I do almost every year—until I had another idea. Holidays be damned, I was going to stay in town and make a movie.

On location in Oklahoma for Cheer for Your life.

A Stalker in the House (2020)

My filmmaker friend Nick Ryan and I were hanging out at my apartment in Sherman Oaks, sipping some Jim Beam, smoking spliffs, and bitching about how the industry shuts down for the holidays. Nicely lit up, we decided we should shoot a movie during the quiet season. It seemed like a great idea at the time. We could film it with my camera and gear and do it entirely in my apartment to save money.

We wanted to rebel against the traditional holiday experience and were determined to find a crew and cast who shared the same mentality. We would also need to find a star name to help us sell the movie; otherwise, making it would be too risky. We knew quite a few stars between the two of us and ended up reaching out to Scout Taylor Compton, an amazing actress whom I'd worked with on *A Daughter's Deceit* and whom Nick had worked with several times. With a star in place, our crazy idea was becoming a reality.

I wrote the script in under ninety-six hours. The writing process was fast and furious, to say the least. I popped a modafinil, drank whiskey, and typed—a lot. It was a blur and a half, but the script turned out solid. The story was about a girl who meets a guy who turns out to be a total psycho. He's a stalker who shows up all the time to stake out her place, kills her friends, and holds her hostage. Of course, she kills him in the end. It wasn't *Lawrence of Arabia*, but for a microbudget, six-day thriller with one location, it was solid.

When we reached out to crew up and hire the rest of the cast, some people told us we were crazy for making a movie over the holidays.

Many people were either out of town, busy, or with family, so we made more calls and before long had assembled a team of talented filmmakers interested in our radical idea.

We would start the shoot a day after Christmas, take New Year's off, and then come back and keep filming. It was a ridiculous schedule, but that was part of the appeal.

Then I started spending money, which made things even more real. I went to Target and bought a shopping cart full of decorations that made my place look like a girl lived there. After I loaded my SUV with pink towels, perfume, and scented candles, I purchased all the various props we would need. All these expenses were adding up, and trust me it feels different when it's coming out of your pocket. You really question whether some purple and pink towels are necessary to sell the character when raggedy, old white towels might be good enough.

I spent a few days completely redesigning my apartment. I cleaned up, hid all my video games, and decorated my spot to look like the character's place. It was surreal going to sleep that night, only to wake up in what looked like a bizarro version of my apartment.

At 6:00 a.m. on day one of the shoot, Nick called and said that Scout Taylor Compton, our lead, had caught COVID and wouldn't be able to work. I panicked. Of course I didn't blame her, but this was bad.

I thought about shutting down the whole thing. Without a star name, it would be nearly impossible to sell the movie. At the same time, though, there was a camera team setting up lights in my living room and people making coffee in my kitchen, getting ready to shoot. I'd hired these people for this crazy idea, and I didn't want to let anyone down. But this was not the day one I had planned! "Fuck!" I shouted at nobody in particular.

Veronica Issa, a talented actress I'd worked with several times, was there to play the role of the best friend over two days of shooting. The obvious solution was to ask Veronica if she would be willing to take over the lead and recast the friend role. I told myself that if Veronica was in and available, we would make the movie, and if not, it wasn't meant to be. I explained the situation to Veronica, and she was happy to take the lead. The decision made itself, and we went on with making the movie. I knew it might be harder to sell, but that was a risk I was willing to take. Reinvigorated, we proceeded.

There was this super-indie vibe on set since the whole thing was in my two-bed apartment. It reminded me of when I was shooting music videos in my mom's house with film school friends. My bedroom was packed with lights on C-stands, and my kitchen became craft services. This was down and dirty. Yet the mood was great, morale was high, Veronica did amazing as the lead, and our small crew was enjoying our version of a filmmaking holiday break. I even jumped into the shot to play one of the supporting roles myself.

Everything was great, and the movie was looking good until neighbor hell started. I anticipated there being some issues, but this got out of hand quickly.

I live in an apartment complex with a clear rule against making movies there. With such a small crew, I thought we could get away with it. We were trying to be as low key as possible, but some of the neighbors had outdoor cameras rolling twenty-four seven.

I started getting phone calls and emails, asking if I was shooting on site. Naturally, I denied it, but it was hard to argue when they were sending me screenshots from their security cameras of the gaffer carrying lights or the camera crew entering with gear. They were also sending me threatening messages, saying they would call the police. If they did that, we were doomed.

Being that we were still in the thick of COVID, I figured I could say my production space in Hollywood had shut down, forcing us to do camera tests in my living room. There was nowhere else to go, I would tell them. It seemed like a pretty realistic scenario, and that clever little lie bought me just enough time to get through the shoot.

I paid $2,500 in fines for making noise and having a vehicle in the driveway, but that was still way cheaper than any location fee.

When the shoot was done, we had a holiday wrap party where we all got shit-faced. The movie received solid reviews and despite not having a star name, Tubi picked it up, and I made money. I call that a win.

In my garage turned movie set, Jack Pearson and Veronica Issa, star in
Stalker in the House.

Lord of the Streets (2021)

My producing partners Demetrius and Ace wanted to step outside of the made-for-TV space and make an action movie with stars. The stakes would be higher because action movies and stars cost more, but it was a risk we were willing to take to level up. When it came time to figure out what script we should do, I remembered something I had written a ways back.

During one of my many writing frenzies, one outline emerged for a fighting movie. I grew up watching karate movies and doing martial arts, and I loved that type of stuff. The script outline had been collecting dust for years—I had to scour through piles of dusty hard drives to even find it. After review, I gave it a nice little update to punch it up.

Demetrius liked what I had. He gave me some notes and told me to write the script, and if he liked it, he was on board to produce it.

I did what I always did: I hunkered down and wrote. I'd wake up, drink coffee, sit down, and write until my face hurt. Every few hours, I would stand up, stretch, and walk around for a few minutes before sitting back down to type. At night I would hit a bowl, crash out, only to wake up and do it all over again. It was my daily schedule until the script was drafted and my preferred method of writing a first draft. Just bang it out.

Once it was drafted, we paid a coverage service three hundred bucks for a professional reader to tear the draft to pieces, and we used their suggestions to make it better. It's good to do this coverage process multiple times. If you think coverage won't help your script, you're probably scared of a professional reader tearing your baby apart. They will, and it's usually for the best. The script greatly improved with their notes. Never forget, the script is everything.

With a solid script in hand, we set out to cast the movie. Since it was a fighting movie, we wanted real UFC fighters. The hard part is getting ahold of these fighters and finding ones that could also act. My producer friend Nick Ryan knew a lot of people, including UFC legend Rampage Jackson, who starred in *The A-Team*. Getting a legitimate UFC superstar to be in our movie was exactly what we needed, so when Rampage's name came up, we jumped all over it.

Rampage told Nick he would look at the script and let us know. That could mean anything, but Nick assured us Rampage was for real. So we waited. When making an offer, you never know how long it's going to take. It could be a few days or a month. It could be never. Thankfully, our wait really was just a few days.

It turned out he was in talks for an upcoming fight, so he wasn't sure if he could do the movie due to training. We coordinated with his team and moved the shoot up to accommodate his schedule. When you have someone like Rampage willing to be in your movie, you make the dates work.

A couple of days after we locked in Rampage, I was out and about in Venice Beach, drinking with my buddy and talking about the upcoming movie. Someone in the group mentioned they happened to know Khalil Rountree Jr., and my ears perked up. I had just watched Khalil fight in the UFC and destroy a guy with one kick. I asked, "Can you give me his number? I might have a movie role for him."

I reached out to Khalil, and he thought the idea of being in a movie would be fun. We auditioned him via Zoom, and he was perfect as one of our leads. We offered him the part straight away, and with two legit UFC fighters in, our little action movie was growing. The movie gods were still smiling on us.

Just as we are finalizing contracts and locations, a producer friend, Evan Forster, said he had a line on Anderson Silva. Again my ears perked up. Anderson "the Spider" Silva is considered one of the greatest fighters to ever live. The man is a UFC legend, and the idea of getting him for the movie was insane.

Evan reassured me that Anderson would be in town in a couple of days and was willing to meet with us if we were serious about making an offer. We assured him we were serious and then set an official time, date, and location for this meeting. Now it was really real. When I entered, "Meeting with Anderson Silva," in my calendar, I couldn't believe it.

Demetrius and I showed up at Evan's slick office on the top floor of a West Hollywood building to meet with Anderson and his manager. We were sharing the usual small talk when the door busted open and the Spider stepped inside. The Brazilian killer radiated this incredible positive energy, instantly putting a smile on my face. I was in awe. We shook hands, and hearing him speak about his love for movies was an experience I will never forget. The man is so nice, but I didn't forget for a moment that he could kick the shit out of all of us in seconds.

A few days later, Demetrius spoke to Anderson's manager and heard he was in. Incredible! We had managed to assemble one hell of a cast: a group of men capable of killing with their bare hands. We also cast Bellator MMA superstar A. J. McKee, UFC star Cheick Kongo, and Brazilian ju-jitsu legend Rigan Machado. We would reunite with hip-hop legend Treach, who starred in my film *Naughty by Nature*, to play our lead hero. It really was a sick cast.

The movie was shaping up to be much cooler than we originally anticipated, but that meant the budget skyrocketed. We asked ourselves whether all of this was really going to make the movie any more valuable. As the budget rose, so did the risk, and that meant the stress went up as well.

Moviemaking is all about thousands of little decisions every day. Things like whether to rent the cheap cop outfits for a couple hundred bucks, saving some money, or spend $2,000 for something more authentic with the full belt. Do we use my cheaper but still cinema-grade lenses, or do we spend a few extra grand and rent anamorphic lenses? Everything makes a difference, but everything also makes the budget go up, and that difference doesn't always add value.

We were spending a lot of money, but we had a much stronger cast than we originally anticipated, so we went all out and agreed to make the movie the best it could be. For our opening fight, we secured a beautiful casino location with a giant ballroom that had massive ceilings and gold chandeliers. It was expensive but needed.

The producer in me didn't want to waste a penny while the director in me wanted the best locations. It was my name on the movie, and I didn't want to make a piece of shit that looked cheap. However, a day before we were set to start shooting at the casino, the workers went on strike, and we lost the location. It took us weeks to find that place and secure it. How the hell would we find another in a day?

Production scrambled, but the only option we found was a sad, white-walled ballroom. White walls, my old nemesis. They always look cheap, and that meant the footage didn't come out nearly as cool as I wanted. It was a mood killer. What could've been a great opening fight didn't look so great.

Watching the white-walled footage back was so painful, we had to reedit the movie to show those scenes in super quick, tight shots. Instead of showing the whole fight, we made the sequence a quick stylized flashback with a heavy color grade to make it work. In a way, doing it like this made the movie more stylized, and even though we were forced into it, I still think it was the right play.

Other than losing the casino, the shoot went great. All our other locations looked authentic, and we even filmed at a real MMA gym in Orange County. Khalil, who had never acted a day in his life, delivered a powerful, raw performance as a convicted murderer. Rampage and Anderson Silva looked badass as boss criminals, and the fights they performed were legit because they are real fighters. Seeing Anderson Silva kick Treach in the head at lightning speed just a few feet away from me is something I'll never forget. As a UFC fan, this was a dream come true.

The movie turned out incredibly well, and it can be viewed exclusively on Tubi. *Lord of the Streets* was certainly a step up for us, and we were happy things were trending that way.

Directing Treach in a fight cage for Lord of the Streets.

Reactor (2021)

I had been pitching and rewriting *Reactor* for a decade. It was my Hail Mary ticket to graduate from the low-budget world and enter the big-budget action movie space. I had written and rewritten fourteen different drafts to get the *Reactor* script in the best shape possible, and at draft fifteen, I convinced my friend and better writer Cam Cannon to do yet another rewrite. Cam dug in and took the script to a whole new level.

During my time trying to get *Reactor* made, I had signed a total of four option agreements with four different production companies. These options were anywhere from six to sixteen months, after which the rights would automatically revert back to me. A producer would express interest, I would sign an option, it would expire, and then I would do the same song and dance with someone else. Many scripts go through this before getting made—it's quite common.

However, in the excitement of signing option agreement after option agreement, I fucked up. I inadvertently optioned the script to two producers at the same time. This put me in a predicament. I had a real producer, Pete, ready to make the movie, but the other producer, Bob, still technically had the rights to the script.

A year earlier, Bob had made promises to rewrite and shop the script. So, going off the strength of Bob's word, I agreed to give him a shot at trying to get the movie made. During that time, Bob had failed to do what he promised. He hadn't even begun a rewrite, but I was still trapped because Pete would not move forward unless Bob signed off on it.

I had to beg and plead for Bob to allow me to make my own movie. Bob had me by the balls, and when all was said and done, I had to give up my backend and a chunk of my paycheck to make him go away peacefully. All the joy of getting this multimillion-dollar movie off the ground was sucked away by one terrible mistake. If I had only waited one more month for Bob's option to expire before signing the next, everything would've been fine and dandy. Fuck it. At least I was about to make *Reactor.* Or so I thought.

Reactor follows an ex-Special Forces guy working in a nuclear power plant that's taken over by bad guys, so the hero has to kick ass and save the day. Pete, the real producer, sent me to Georgia to get preproduction underway. By the time I landed, I was already excited to make this movie. We start looking for a location to double as a nuclear power plant. Well, it turns out that finding a nuclear power plant in Georgia or anywhere else was much harder than I'd anticipated.

It was a struggle to secure a location, and I kept coming up short. We couldn't find a power plant or anywhere that could even double as a power plant. As more time passed, not being able to get a location put the movie in real jeopardy—so much so that when local producers were presented with the option of using an abandoned meat factory, I was coming up with creative ways to make it work.

It turned out the abandoned meat factory would not satisfy Pete, and I was instructed to go back home to Los Angeles. I was sure that *Reactor* would never get made. I felt sick. It was not a joyful holiday break.

I sat at home feeling miserable, having already told my family I was doing a big movie. Now they were asking me about the movie around the dinner table, and I had no good answers. Things were bleak until a producer in Georgia found a hydroelectric dam that was extremely cinematic. A glimmer of hope. The producer called and asked if I could rewrite the story to take place at a dam instead of a nuclear power plant. You bet I could! Never before was I so elated to rewrite a script. A rewrite meant there was hope again, so I dug in and researched hydroelectric plants before getting to work.

Hope can be a dangerous thing. This producer had warned me that the location may or may not get approved—it partially depended on the rewrite. That meant there was a chance I would rewrite the script only for it to get passed over, but hope was what I needed. I needed to believe the movie could work, or else the rewrite would suffer.

Some tweaking is usually necessary after location scouting so what's on the page matches what you actually have. Houses turn into apartments, and offices turn into coffee shops. But turning a nuclear power plant into a dam was a bit more work. I did not procrastinate. I hunkered down and wrote, or rather rewrote.

To my surprise, the rewrite worked, and in some ways, the script came out better. Instead of the bad guy threatening to melt down a nuclear plant, he could now open floodgates and cause some real destruction while immediately killing people. The buildup was scarier, with more violence and suspense. I sent in the new script and prayed. Days passed, and I heard nothing; I was sure a hydroelectric dam would never get approved if they thought they were getting a movie about a nuclear power plant. Then my phone rang with good news.

The movie was officially back on track, and then Pete gave me the truly amazing news: he had secured movie star Bruce Willis to be our main bad guy. I was ecstatic. Bruce was the biggest name I'd had the privilege to direct.

I got my ass back on a plane to Georgia and marched up to the dam. It was a fantastic find. The place was a marvel of engineering with all sorts of interesting machinery. That night, we all had a big dinner for production. It was so special to see the team talking about what we were all there to do. We were shooting *Reactor*. The word *reactor* had been bouncing inside my head for so long—this truly was a dream come true. I finally felt as if I was a tiny bit more than semi successful.

The locals who worked at the dam were super helpful. These guys were the real deal, hard-working, blue-collar Georgia men who kept the place running. We cast them in the movie as extras, and they even opened the floodgates for us. Watching forty thousand gallons of water pour through each second was incredible. Giant rods were spinning so fast that if you touched them, your arm would get ripped right off your body.

Production put me up at a gorgeous lakeside villa—a far cry from the cheap hotels I usually frequented. The crew started showing up, and production was getting into full swing. We had taken over the entire resort, and the place was abuzz with the feeling that *Reactor* was a big deal. There were more people, more trucks, more equipment, and more money than many of us were used to.

I was preparing myself, spending a lot of time at the dam with the DP, AD, and stunt coordinator, walking through scenes and doing prep work without having the actors with us. As we got closer to the shoot date, I was getting anxious. This was by far my biggest movie, and I didn't want it to suck. I spent every night going over the script, making notes, drawing up shots, and thinking of ways to make the movie good while putting my stamp on it.

On day one, I drove up and saw trailers and trucks lined down the block. I've driven past productions with rows of trailers and trucks like that and always fantasized about helming a big movie like that. Well, here I was.

After my Red Bull kicked in, we started working, and in those first moments, I realized the size of the budget didn't matter. Filmmaking is filmmaking. Bigger-budget shoots have more toys and more expensive faces, but the mechanics are the same. I realized I could do a studio movie. I knew I could because there I was, doing a bigger movie and doing it well.

My cinematographer, Brandon Cox, was right there beside me, creating stunning images on Red Geminis with premium Cooke anamorphic lenses. Everything was top of the line.

We did some of the most complex stunts I have ever done, the most challenging being one where Patrick Muldoon, the hero, is hiding out under the dam. Patrick's character shoots a guy on the dam, who then falls into the water before Patrick scales up the side of the dam and takes out yet another guy. You have to understand, this dam is very tall, and falling off it meant instant death. Not movie dead, for-real dead.

Between all the complex rigging, coordination, and safety precautions, that one stunt took a day and a half to shoot—longer than I'd ever had the luxury of spending on a stunt sequence. We pulled it off, it looked great, and nobody got hurt. The only thing that fell in the water was Patrick's phone, and production got him a new one.

Then Bruce showed up like a boss on a private jet with his team. The whole town went nuts, with reporters and townspeople showing up, snapping photos. Having a legit movie star on the set raises the bar for everyone else. Bruce killed it as the bad guy, giving a fantastic, menacing performance.

We stayed on schedule and on budget, and when it was all in the can, we went to the bar at the resort to celebrate. The next day, I flew back to Los Angeles, hungover and once again unemployed. This time, though, I wasn't freaking out. I'd leveled up. I'd taken on a whole new challenge. I'd made it.

I knew when we couldn't find a nuclear power plant, the movie title would get changed. The movie was released as *Deadlock*—a catchy title, but it will always be *Reactor* to me.

With the legend Bruce Willis on the set of Deadlock.

Vendetta (2022)

Shortly after *Reactor* wrapped, I was speaking with Pete, the producer, about doing another action movie. He liked what I did with *Reactor* and was down to work with me again. This was exactly where I wanted to be, doing bigger-budget movies with bigger stars.

The problem was I didn't have another script, and being a movie director without a script is like trying to sell sandwiches without bread. I certainly didn't want to wait for him to call me, so I decided the only logical thing to do was bang out another script that was right for him. I dove into writing a revenge action movie called *Blood for Blood*.

I had a rough script and was finalizing the editing on *Reactor* when my phone rang. It was Pete. He asked if I had another script, and I decided to hell with it—I would send him the new script without anyone reading it first. However, the second I hit send I was consumed with regret. I should've waited! The first draft can't be good, and people never give a script a second look. I'd fucked it all up.

My best move was to email Pete and tell him not to read the script yet. I composed the message, but staring right back at me was the attached script from my last email. Maybe it was a good first draft. Maybe I had nothing to worry about. As I opened the script to reread, it dawned on me that it didn't matter what I thought. Sending Pete a back-peddling email would be amateurish. I closed my laptop and let the movie gods decide.

A week later I got a phone call from Pete. Not only did he read it, but so did a major sales company and distributor—and they both loved it. It felt amazing to hear, and what felt better was Pete telling me he got the picture greenlit to start shooting in a couple of months. This type of shit never happens. It's the Hollywood dream.

It kept getting better when he told me Mike Tyson, Thomas Jane, Theo Rossi, and Clive Standen would be in the movie. This cast was on a whole new level for me, and I would also be reuniting with Bruce Willis, which was even better. These actors were heavyweights, respectable performers, and I was directing them. I was leveling up again, and it was definitely a good feeling. As a perk, there was no nuclear power plant to find.

I flew back to Georgia for the production of *Blood for Blood*, now officially called *Vendetta*. We went to a small rural town called Eatonton, where a man named Jim Stone runs everything film related. Jim purchased an abandoned jail from the town and turned it into production offices and a filming location. The man loves filmmaking, and we had full run of the town because of him. When you bring a big show with famous faces to a small town, that's a big deal, and it showed.

When the actors started showing up, that was when I knew there was no going back. Thomas Jane's character was a transient type who resided in motels doing shady business. The man is a star, and production searched for the finest accommodations in town, but Jane wanted to stay at the seedy motel like his character. A method-acting approach. I loved it. We rolled up, and there he was, smoking a pipe with no shoes on, already getting into character.

284

Thomas had prepared a whole backstory about his character being a grifter, and hearing him detail his thoughts was fascinating. He had even considered his character's family and relationships with other characters. He knew the script inside and out.

Then when Mike Tyson showed up, everyone showed up. The man is arguably one of the most famous people in the world, and he draws a crowd. When the cameras were rolling, Mike was a gritty gangster who stole cars and sold guns. We had to have him punch someone out in the movie, and I swear I've never seen anyone punch so fast.

On one of the last days, I looked up and saw a group of people from the Make-a-Wish Foundation. They were escorting a disabled and terminally ill young man, Bobby Hill, in his wheelchair onto the set. Upon meeting Bobby, a wave of emotion went through me. He had a beautiful smile, and although he was not able to speak, he communicated everything with his eyes. I made sure everyone on the set treated him as a VIP. He sat next to me at video village and had a front-row seat to view some moviemaking in action. It was a great experience for all of us, and I hope I helped to brighten that one day for him.

With Bobby Hill and star of Vendetta Clive Standen.

Lastly

These days I'm in postproduction on a movie called *The Getback*, which we just shot in Mississippi. I was there for a month. We had a good budget, flipped cars, had epic gunfights, and sent people jumping off balconies. It was rad. There are talks about a *Lord of the Streets 2*, and if that's what the platforms want, that is what I shall do. You can't predict the deal; you can only play the cards you're dealt.

Although I'm concluding the book, my journey continues. I came a long way, but it took a long time and a lot of pain. I may never get the chance to work with major studios or A-list stars, but I've given up the notion that I must get to that place to be content. If you are constantly disappointed with where you are in life, you will never be a happy camper.

There's no formula to success. In this business, there's no rhyme or reason why things happen. You may never feel successful. I've been at this for twenty years, and for me, there is no off button. I simply don't know how to stop. I had to endure the fire to get to where I am because I had no other option, and I'm still not where I want to be.

My advice is to do the best work you can. At the end of the day, filmmaking is about telling a great story for other people to enjoy, so tell great stories. The work really is the only thing that should matter. And never compare yourself to others in the industry. There's always someone else doing way better.

The best piece of advice I can give you is to be born with rich and famous parents. For the rest of us, just keep going. Stopping means you're as good as dead. So, to everyone just scraping by, anxious, down and out, and doing everything to catch a break—keep going. Keep working on that script and shooting things, improve your craft, and hopefully things will work out. I can't guarantee you'll succeed, but I can guarantee if you stop, you never will.

I hope my stories and ramblings were informative, helpful, or at least entertaining. It's been quite the adventure, and I don't plan on stopping anytime soon. And who knows, I might see you out there.

Writing this book was a lot like writing a script but with way more words. I have to call it complete before I can send it out. Just like everything else I've written, I'll look it over one more time, and when it's good and ready, I'll hit send.

THE END

Follow me @jaredcohn1
Thanks for reading.

Ingram Content Group UK Ltd.
Milton Keynes UK
UKHW020728170523
421890UK00015B/463